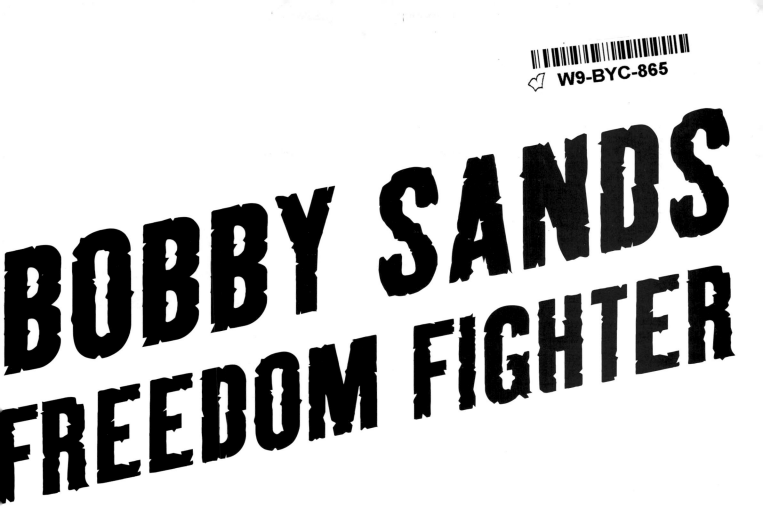

BOBBY SANDS
FREEDOM FIGHTER

Written & Drawn by
GERRY HUNT

Coloured by
MATT GRIFFIN

THE O'BRIEN PRESS
DUBLIN

This edition first published 2016 by
The O'Brien Press Ltd,
12 Terenure Road East, Rathgar,
Dublin 6, D06 HD27, Ireland.
Tel: +353 1 4923333; Fax: +353 1 4922777
E-mail: books@obrien.ie.
Website: www.obrien.ie

ISBN: 978-1-84717-815-2

Colourist: Matthew Griffin

1 3 5 7 6 4 2
16 18 20 19 17

Printed and bound in Poland by Białostockie Zakłady Graficzne S.A.
The paper in this book is produced using pulp from managed forests.

arts council of Northern Ireland

LOTTERY FUNDED

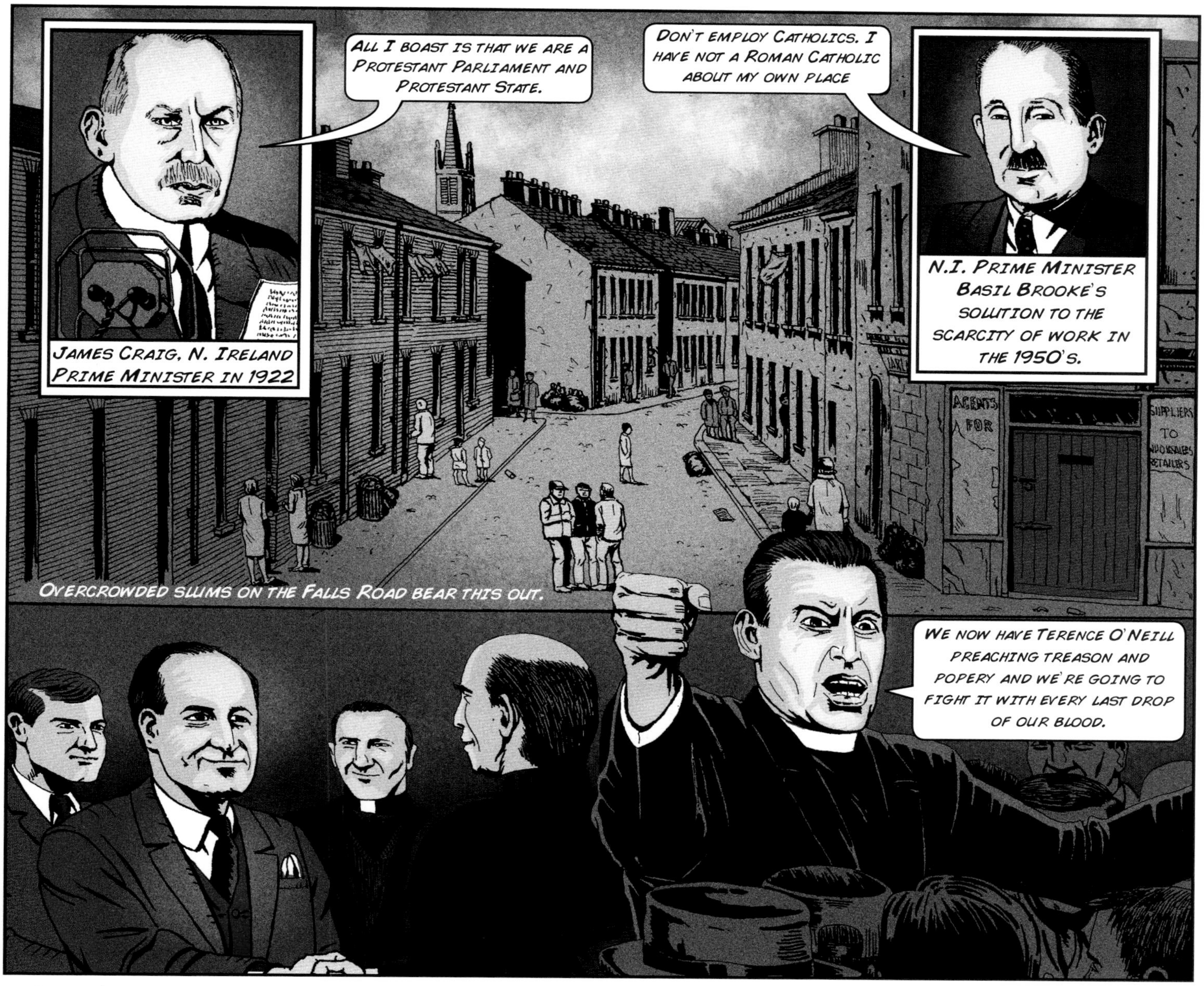
ALL I BOAST IS THAT WE ARE A PROTESTANT PARLIAMENT AND PROTESTANT STATE.
JAMES CRAIG, N. IRELAND PRIME MINISTER IN 1922
DON'T EMPLOY CATHOLICS. I HAVE NOT A ROMAN CATHOLIC ABOUT MY OWN PLACE
N.I. PRIME MINISTER BASIL BROOKE'S SOLUTION TO THE SCARCITY OF WORK IN THE 1950'S.
AGENTS FOR
SUPPLIERS TO
OVERCROWDED SLUMS ON THE FALLS ROAD BEAR THIS OUT.
WE NOW HAVE TERENCE O'NEILL PREACHING TREASON AND POPERY AND WE'RE GOING TO FIGHT IT WITH EVERY LAST DROP OF OUR BLOOD.

BROOKE'S SUCCESSOR, TERENCE O'NEILL, WAS MORE LIBERAL, VISITING CATHOLIC SCHOOLS AND SPEAKING OF REFORMS IN 1966. THE REV. IAN PAISLEY, HEAD OF THE FREE PRESBYTERIAN CHURCH, REACTED QUICKLY TO THIS.

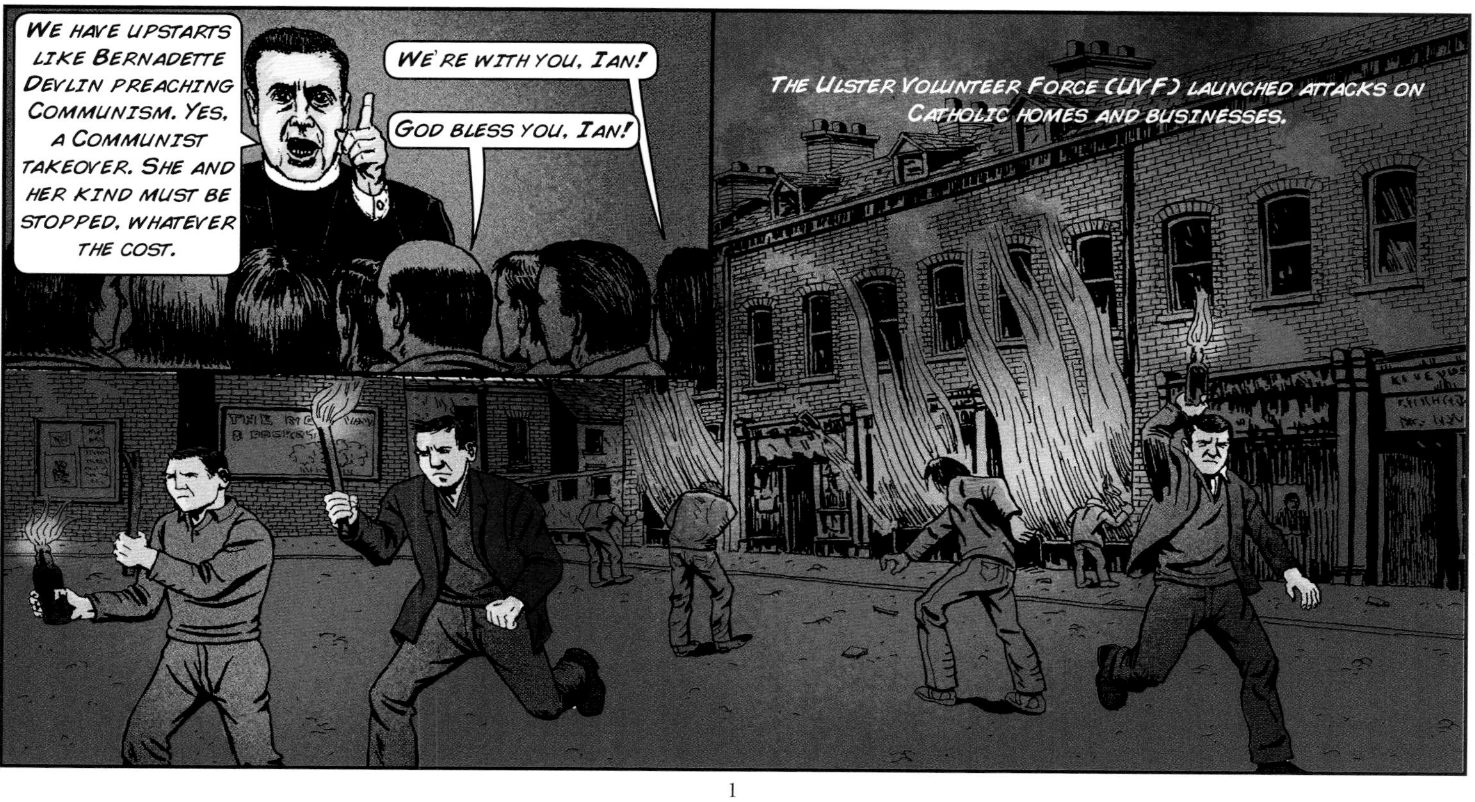
WE HAVE UPSTARTS LIKE BERNADETTE DEVLIN PREACHING COMMUNISM. YES, A COMMUNIST TAKEOVER. SHE AND HER KIND MUST BE STOPPED, WHATEVER THE COST.
WE'RE WITH YOU, IAN!
GOD BLESS YOU, IAN!
THE ULSTER VOLUNTEER FORCE (UVF) LAUNCHED ATTACKS ON CATHOLIC HOMES AND BUSINESSES.

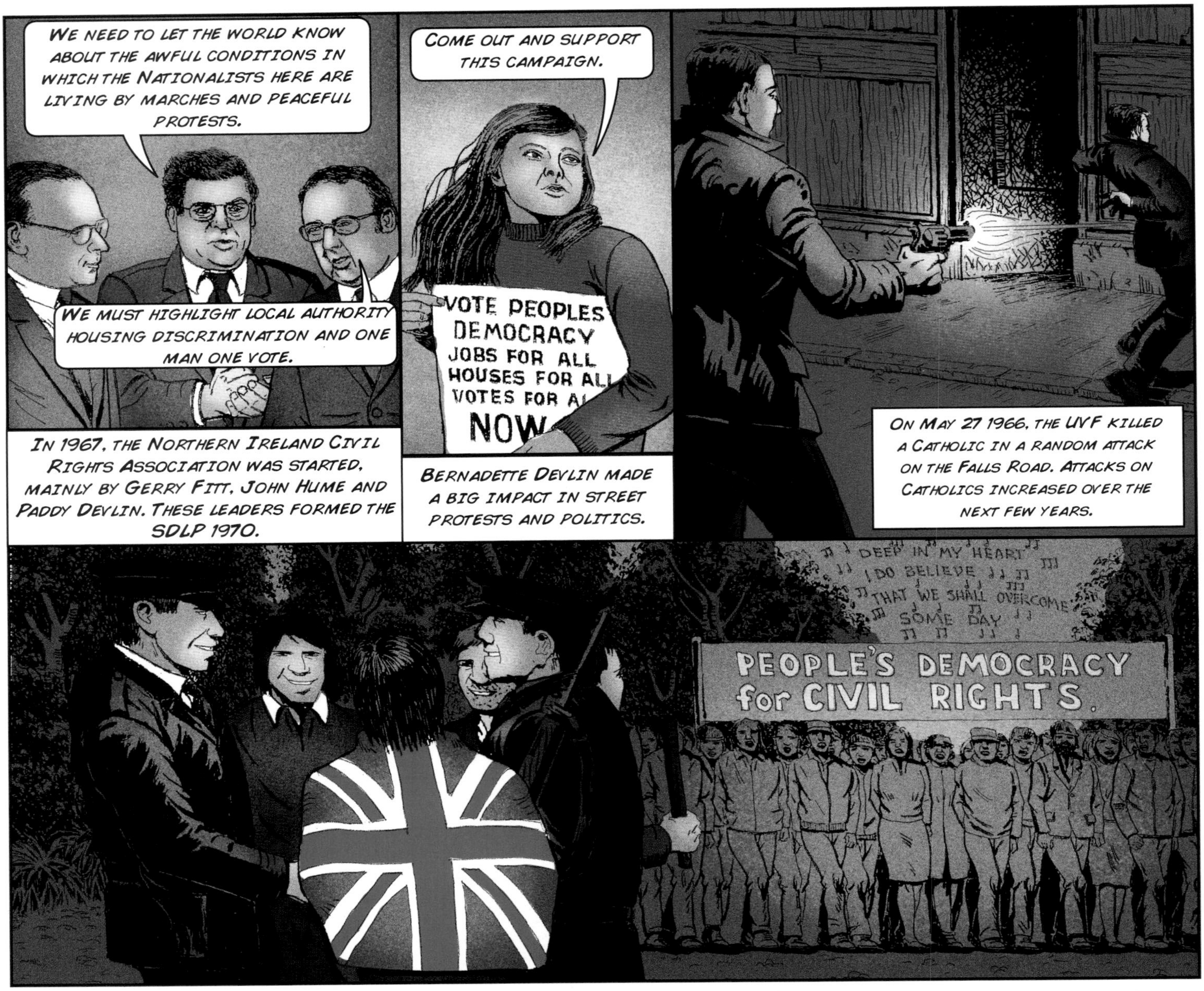
WE NEED TO LET THE WORLD KNOW ABOUT THE AWFUL CONDITIONS IN WHICH THE NATIONALISTS HERE ARE LIVING BY MARCHES AND PEACEFUL PROTESTS.
WE MUST HIGHLIGHT LOCAL AUTHORITY HOUSING DISCRIMINATION AND ONE MAN ONE VOTE.
IN 1967, THE NORTHERN IRELAND CIVIL RIGHTS ASSOCIATION WAS STARTED, MAINLY BY GERRY FITT, JOHN HUME AND PADDY DEVLIN. THESE LEADERS FORMED THE SDLP 1970.
COME OUT AND SUPPORT THIS CAMPAIGN.
VOTE PEOPLES DEMOCRACY JOBS FOR ALL HOUSES FOR ALL VOTES FOR A NOW
BERNADETTE DEVLIN MADE A BIG IMPACT IN STREET PROTESTS AND POLITICS.
ON MAY 27 1966, THE UVF KILLED A CATHOLIC IN A RANDOM ATTACK ON THE FALLS ROAD. ATTACKS ON CATHOLICS INCREASED OVER THE NEXT FEW YEARS.
DEEP IN MY HEART
I DO BELIEVE
THAT WE SHALL OVERCOME
SOME DAY
PEOPLE'S DEMOCRACY for CIVIL RIGHTS.

IN 1969, A GROUP OF STUDENTS, THE PEOPLE'S DEMOCRACY FROM QUEEN'S UNIVERSITY, SET OFF ON A CIVIL RIGHTS MARCH FROM BELFAST TO DERRY. THEY WERE AMBUSHED REPEATEDLY BY THE UVF WHO WERE SEEN TALKING AMICABLY TO THE RUC. AT BURNTOLLET BRIDGE OUTSIDE DERRY CITY...

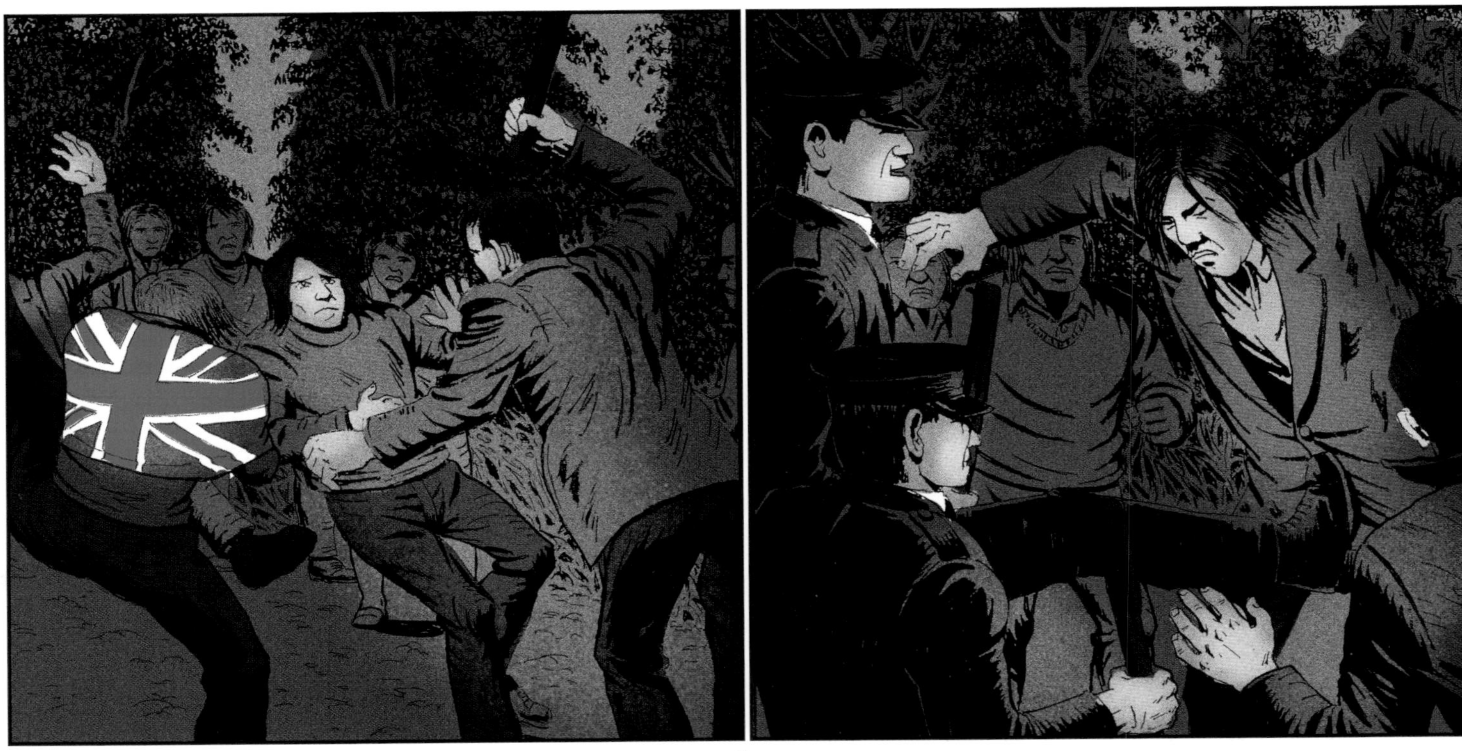

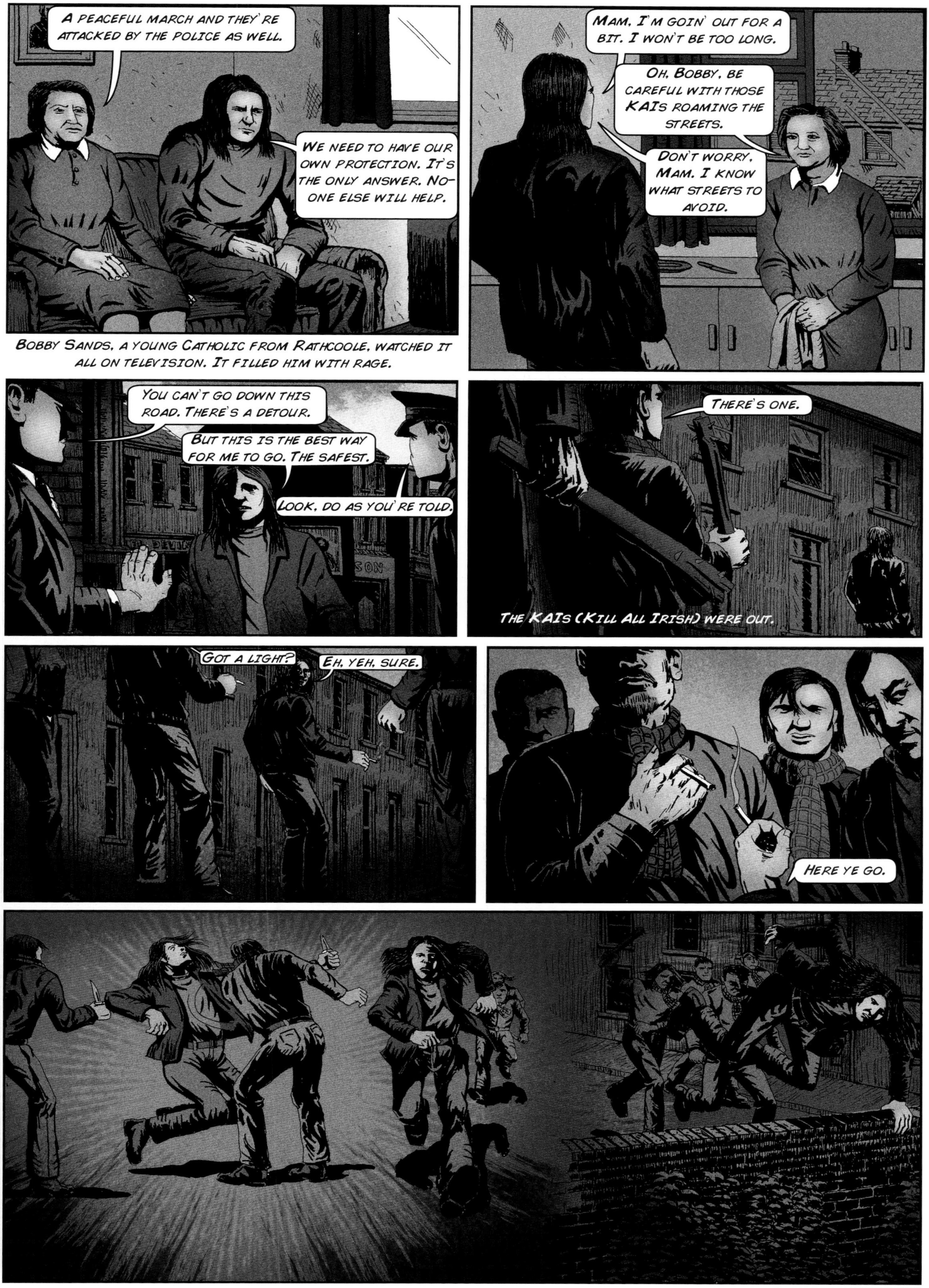
A PEACEFUL MARCH AND THEY'RE ATTACKED BY THE POLICE AS WELL.
WE NEED TO HAVE OUR OWN PROTECTION. IT'S THE ONLY ANSWER. NO-ONE ELSE WILL HELP.
BOBBY SANDS, A YOUNG CATHOLIC FROM RATHCOOLE, WATCHED IT ALL ON TELEVISION. IT FILLED HIM WITH RAGE.
MAM, I'M GOIN' OUT FOR A BIT. I WON'T BE TOO LONG.
OH, BOBBY, BE CAREFUL WITH THOSE KAIs ROAMING THE STREETS.
DON'T WORRY, MAM. I KNOW WHAT STREETS TO AVOID.
YOU CAN'T GO DOWN THIS ROAD. THERE'S A DETOUR.
BUT THIS IS THE BEST WAY FOR ME TO GO. THE SAFEST.
LOOK, DO AS YOU'RE TOLD.
THERE'S ONE.
THE KAIs (KILL ALL IRISH) WERE OUT.
GOT A LIGHT?
EH, YEH, SURE.
HERE YE GO.

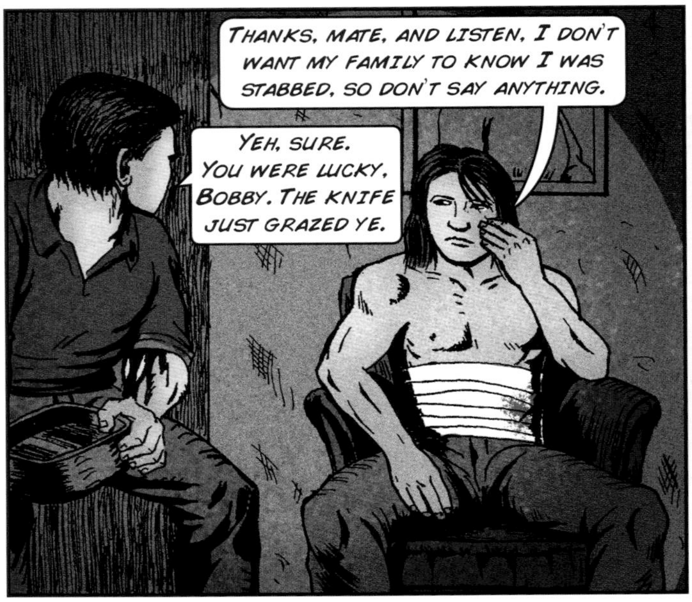
Thanks, mate, and listen. I don't want my family to know I was stabbed, so don't say anything.
Yeh, sure. You were lucky, Bobby. The knife just grazed ye.

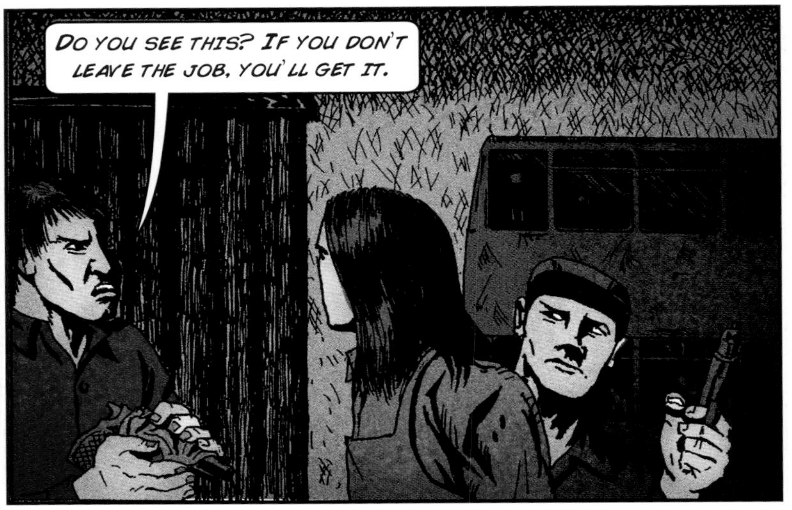
Do you see this? If you don't leave the job, you'll get it.

Bobby, an apprentice coach builder, was getting threats from the Loyalist workforce, which he ignored, but he was finally laid off by the boss on the pretext of the need to reduce staff.

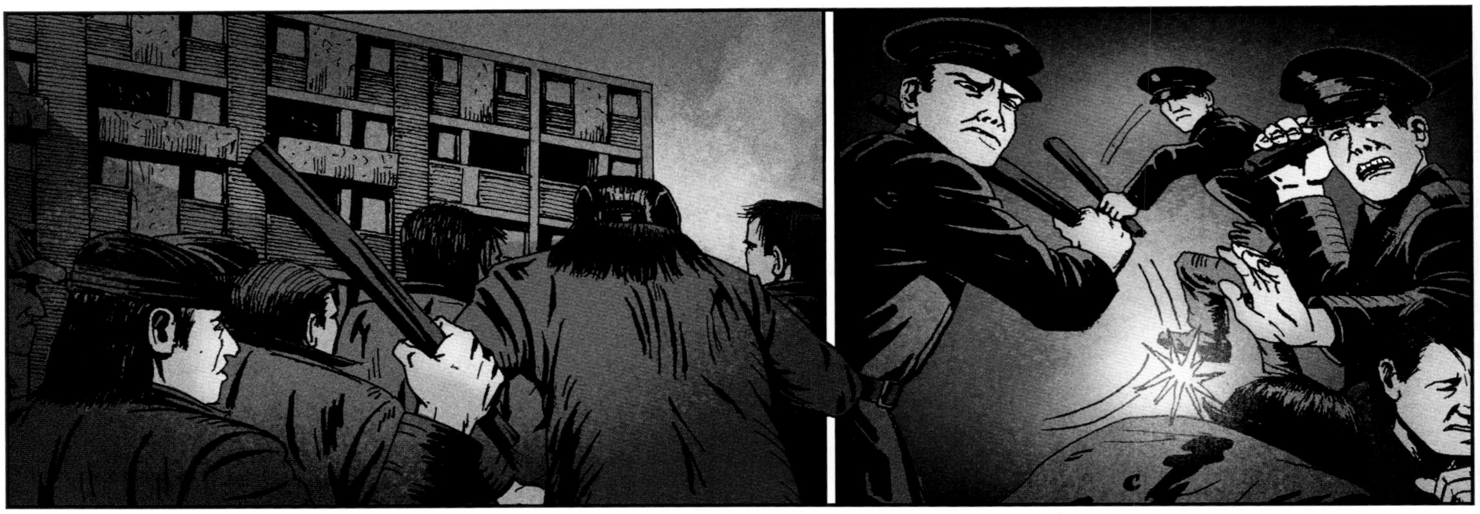

In August, a gang of Loyalists attacked Unity Flats, Belfast. The Catholics resisted and the RUC went on a violent rampage against them, beating one Catholic man to death. The IRA were doing nothing to protect them.

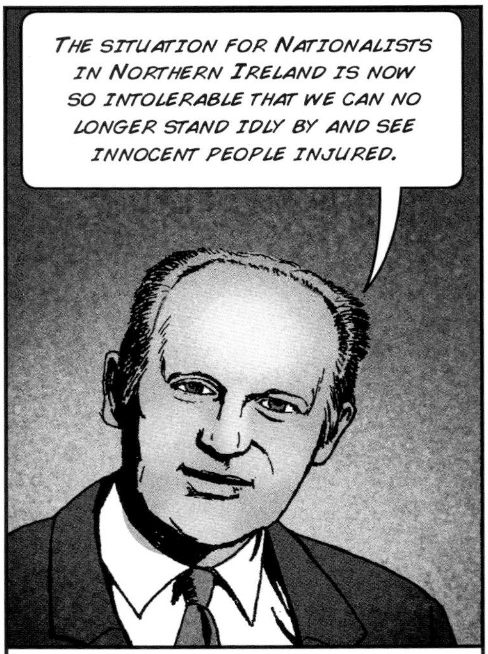
The situation for Nationalists in Northern Ireland is now so intolerable that we can no longer stand idly by and see innocent people injured.

The Nationalists in the North were now being so badly treated that Jack Lynch, the Taoiseach of the Irish Republic, addressed the nation on television.

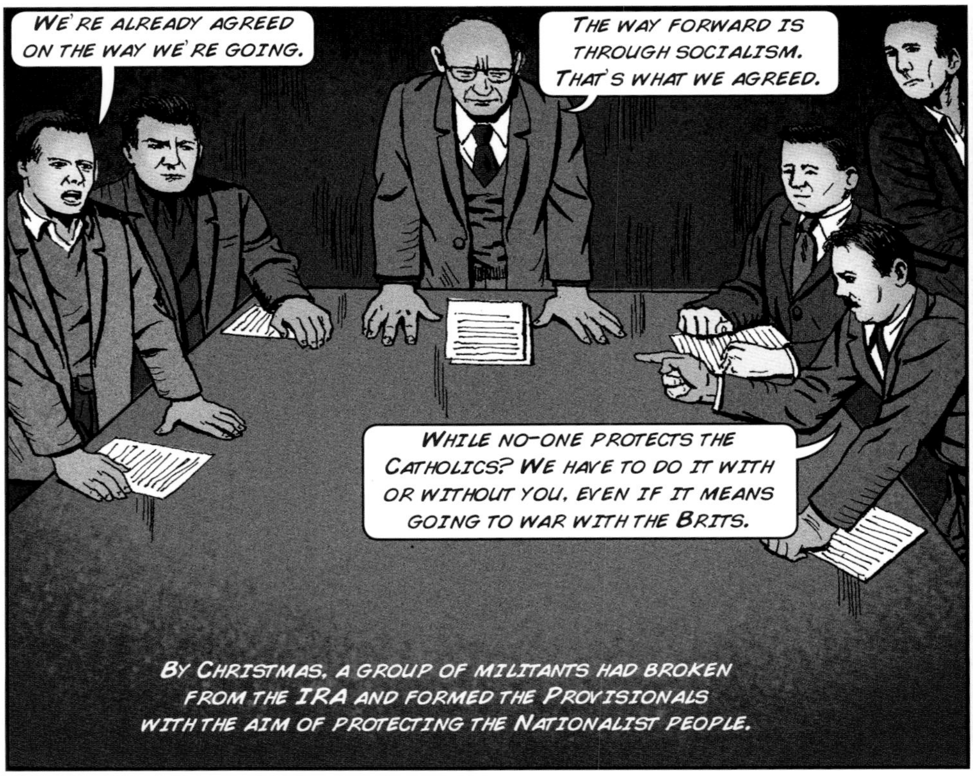
We're already agreed on the way we're going.
The way forward is through socialism. That's what we agreed.
While no-one protects the Catholics? We have to do it with or without you, even if it means going to war with the Brits.

By Christmas, a group of militants had broken from the IRA and formed the Provisionals with the aim of protecting the Nationalist people.

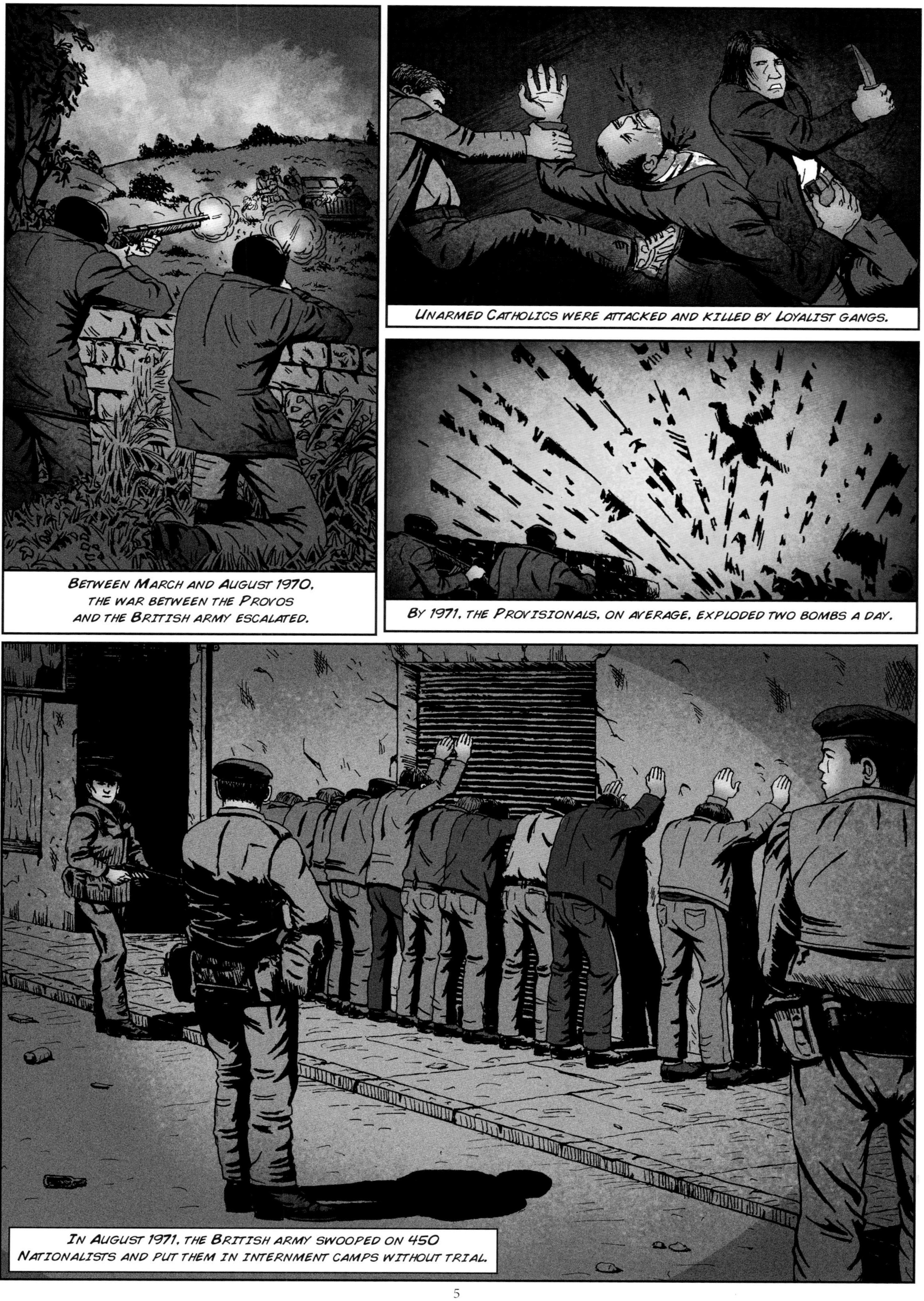
BETWEEN MARCH AND AUGUST 1970, THE WAR BETWEEN THE PROVOS AND THE BRITISH ARMY ESCALATED.
UNARMED CATHOLICS WERE ATTACKED AND KILLED BY LOYALIST GANGS.
BY 1971, THE PROVISIONALS, ON AVERAGE, EXPLODED TWO BOMBS A DAY.
IN AUGUST 1971, THE BRITISH ARMY SWOOPED ON 450 NATIONALISTS AND PUT THEM IN INTERNMENT CAMPS WITHOUT TRIAL.

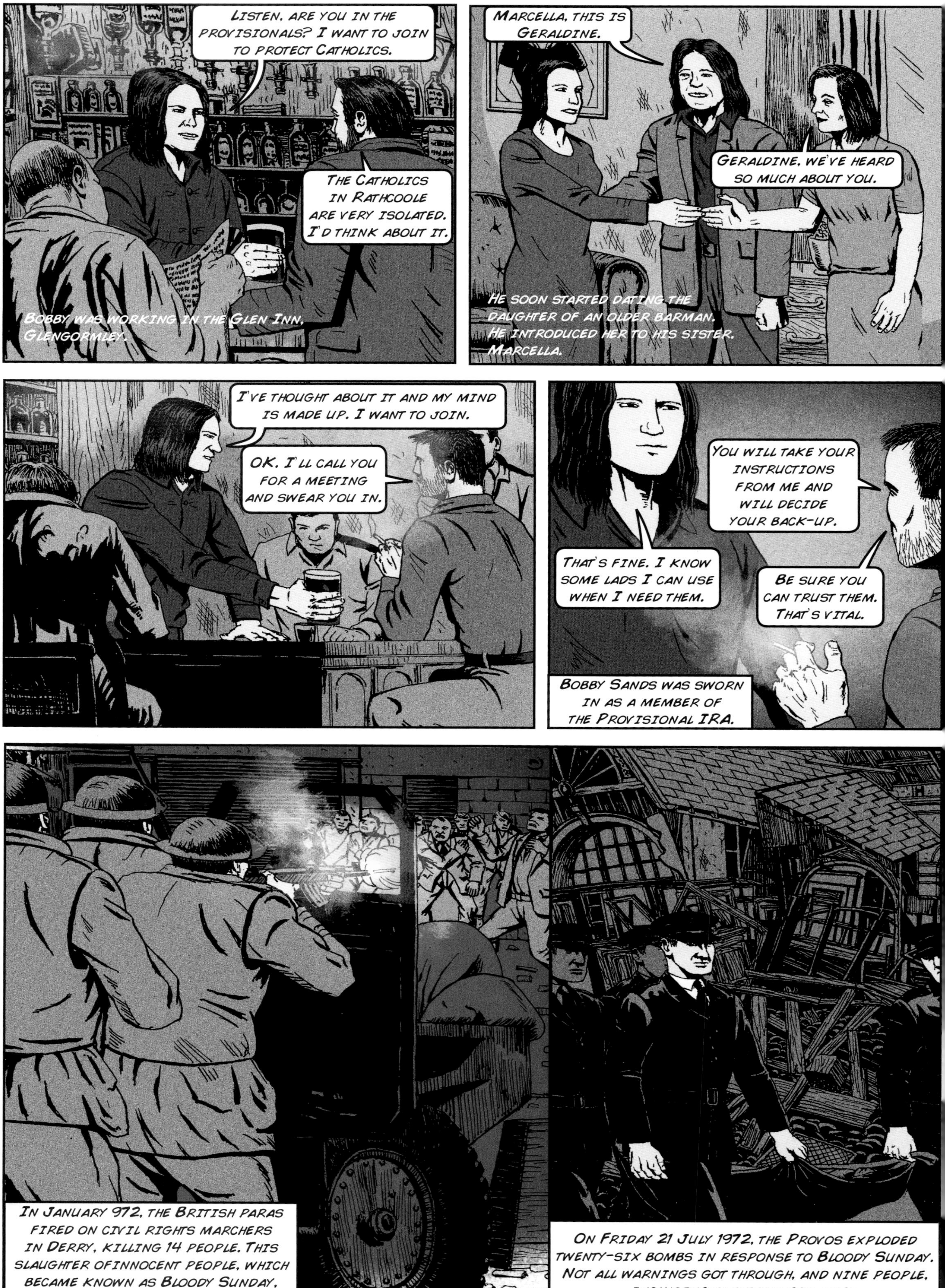
LISTEN, ARE YOU IN THE PROVISIONALS? I WANT TO JOIN TO PROTECT CATHOLICS.
THE CATHOLICS IN RATHCOOLE ARE VERY ISOLATED. I'D THINK ABOUT IT.
BOBBY WAS WORKING IN THE GLEN INN, GLENGORMLEY.
MARCELLA, THIS IS GERALDINE.
GERALDINE, WE'VE HEARD SO MUCH ABOUT YOU.
HE SOON STARTED DATING THE DAUGHTER OF AN OLDER BARMAN. HE INTRODUCED HER TO HIS SISTER, MARCELLA.
I'VE THOUGHT ABOUT IT AND MY MIND IS MADE UP. I WANT TO JOIN.
OK. I'LL CALL YOU FOR A MEETING AND SWEAR YOU IN.
YOU WILL TAKE YOUR INSTRUCTIONS FROM ME AND WILL DECIDE YOUR BACK-UP.
THAT'S FINE. I KNOW SOME LADS I CAN USE WHEN I NEED THEM.
BE SURE YOU CAN TRUST THEM. THAT'S VITAL.
BOBBY SANDS WAS SWORN IN AS A MEMBER OF THE PROVISIONAL IRA.
IN JANUARY 972, THE BRITISH PARAS FIRED ON CIVIL RIGHTS MARCHERS IN DERRY, KILLING 14 PEOPLE. THIS SLAUGHTER OFINNOCENT PEOPLE, WHICH BECAME KNOWN AS BLOODY SUNDAY, CAUSED WORLDWIDE REVULSION.
ON FRIDAY 21 JULY 1972, THE PROVOS EXPLODED TWENTY-SIX BOMBS IN RESPONSE TO BLOODY SUNDAY. NOT ALL WARNINGS GOT THROUGH, AND NINE PEOPLE, INCLUDING TWO SOLDIERS, DIED.

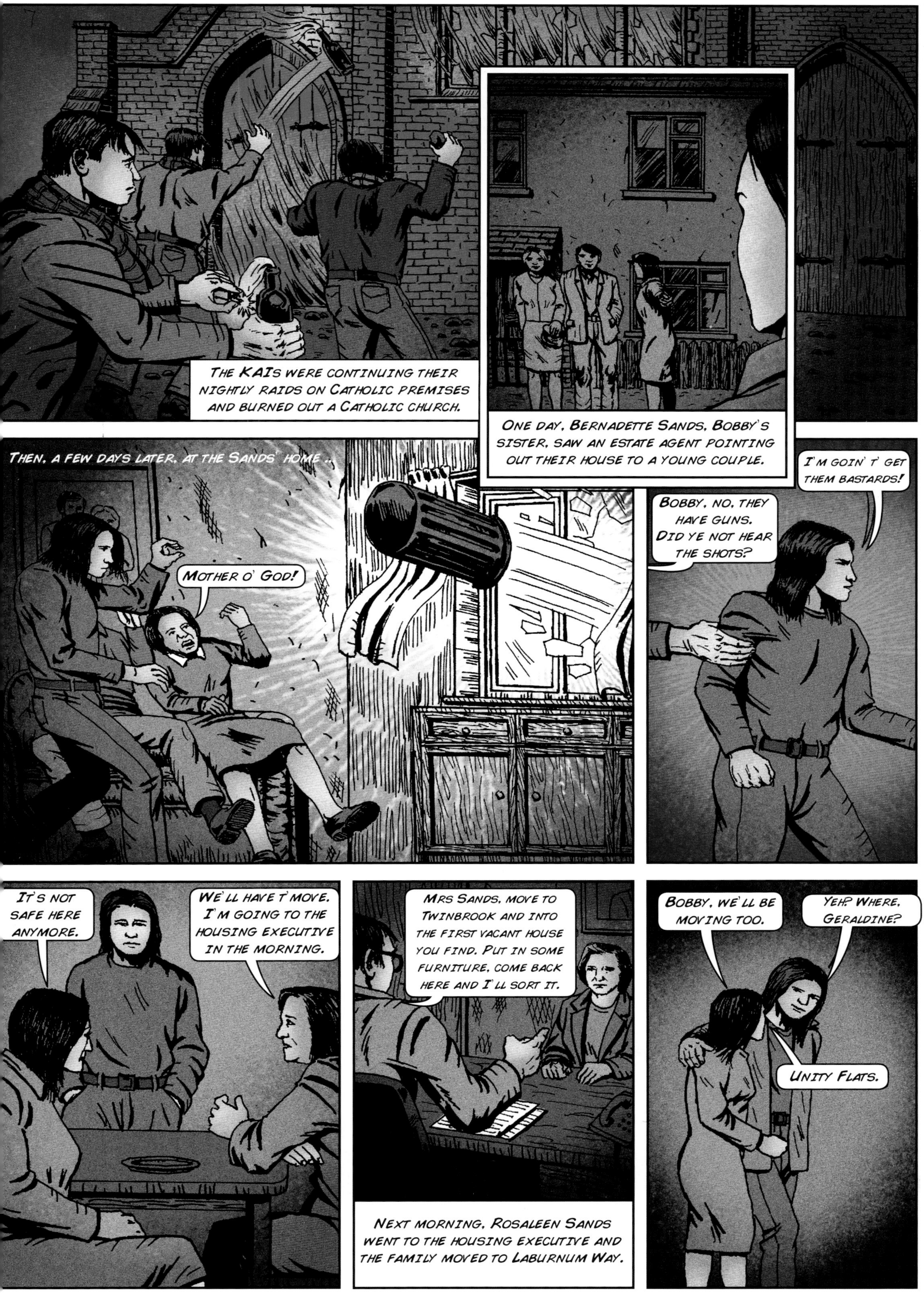

THE KAIs WERE CONTINUING THEIR NIGHTLY RAIDS ON CATHOLIC PREMISES AND BURNED OUT A CATHOLIC CHURCH.
ONE DAY, BERNADETTE SANDS, BOBBY'S SISTER, SAW AN ESTATE AGENT POINTING OUT THEIR HOUSE TO A YOUNG COUPLE.
THEN, A FEW DAYS LATER, AT THE SANDS' HOME ...
MOTHER O' GOD!
I'M GOIN' T' GET THEM BASTARDS!
BOBBY, NO, THEY HAVE GUNS. DID YE NOT HEAR THE SHOTS?
IT'S NOT SAFE HERE ANYMORE.
WE'LL HAVE T' MOVE. I'M GOING TO THE HOUSING EXECUTIVE IN THE MORNING.
MRS SANDS, MOVE TO TWINBROOK AND INTO THE FIRST VACANT HOUSE YOU FIND. PUT IN SOME FURNITURE, COME BACK HERE AND I'LL SORT IT.
NEXT MORNING, ROSALEEN SANDS WENT TO THE HOUSING EXECUTIVE AND THE FAMILY MOVED TO LABURNUM WAY.
BOBBY, WE'LL BE MOVING TOO.
YEH? WHERE, GERALDINE?
UNITY FLATS.

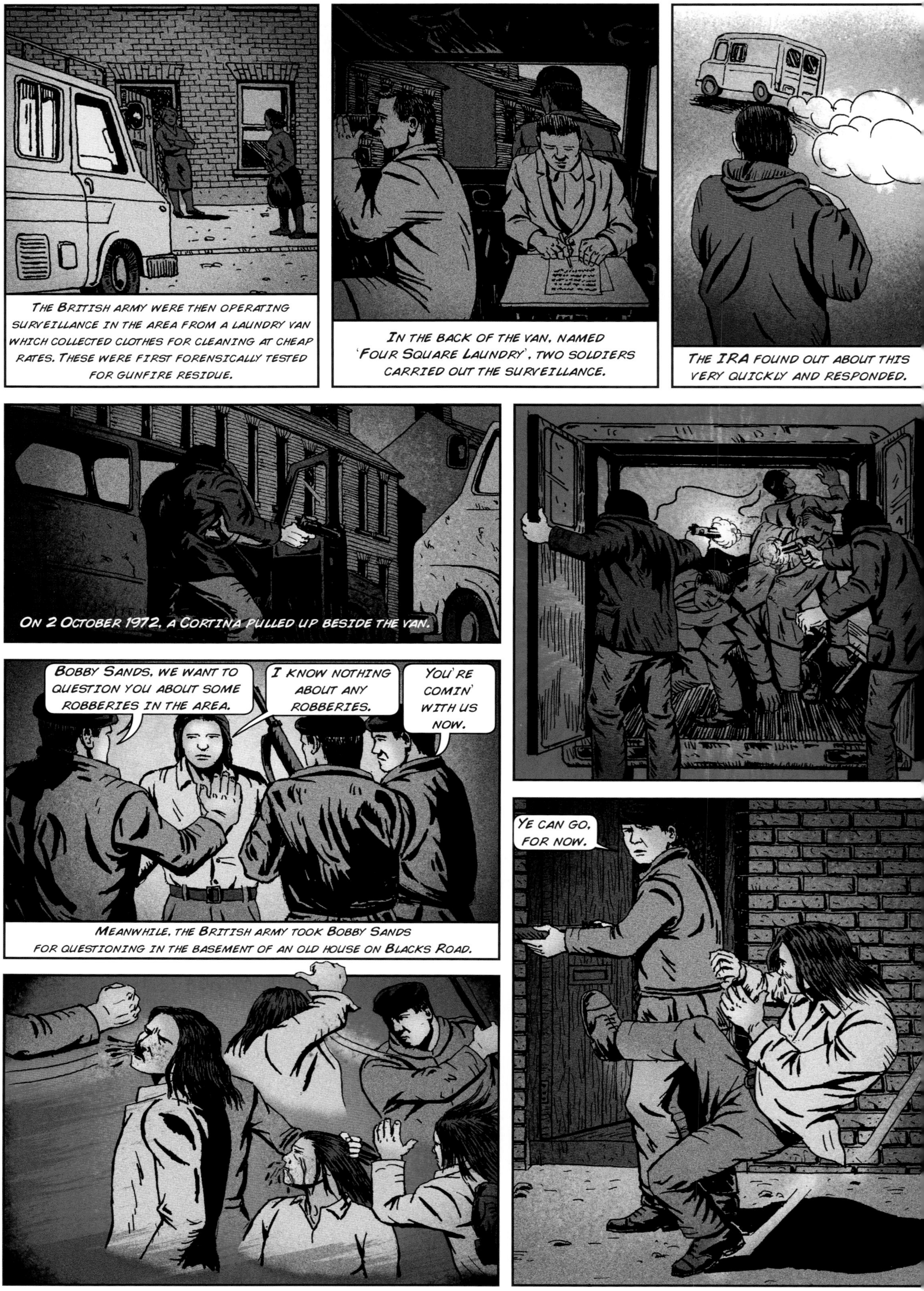
THE BRITISH ARMY WERE THEN OPERATING SURVEILLANCE IN THE AREA FROM A LAUNDRY VAN WHICH COLLECTED CLOTHES FOR CLEANING AT CHEAP RATES. THESE WERE FIRST FORENSICALLY TESTED FOR GUNFIRE RESIDUE.
IN THE BACK OF THE VAN, NAMED 'FOUR SQUARE LAUNDRY', TWO SOLDIERS CARRIED OUT THE SURVEILLANCE.
THE IRA FOUND OUT ABOUT THIS VERY QUICKLY AND RESPONDED.
ON 2 OCTOBER 1972, A CORTINA PULLED UP BESIDE THE VAN.
BOBBY SANDS, WE WANT TO QUESTION YOU ABOUT SOME ROBBERIES IN THE AREA.
I KNOW NOTHING ABOUT ANY ROBBERIES.
YOU'RE COMIN' WITH US NOW.
MEANWHILE, THE BRITISH ARMY TOOK BOBBY SANDS FOR QUESTIONING IN THE BASEMENT OF AN OLD HOUSE ON BLACKS ROAD.
YE CAN GO, FOR NOW.

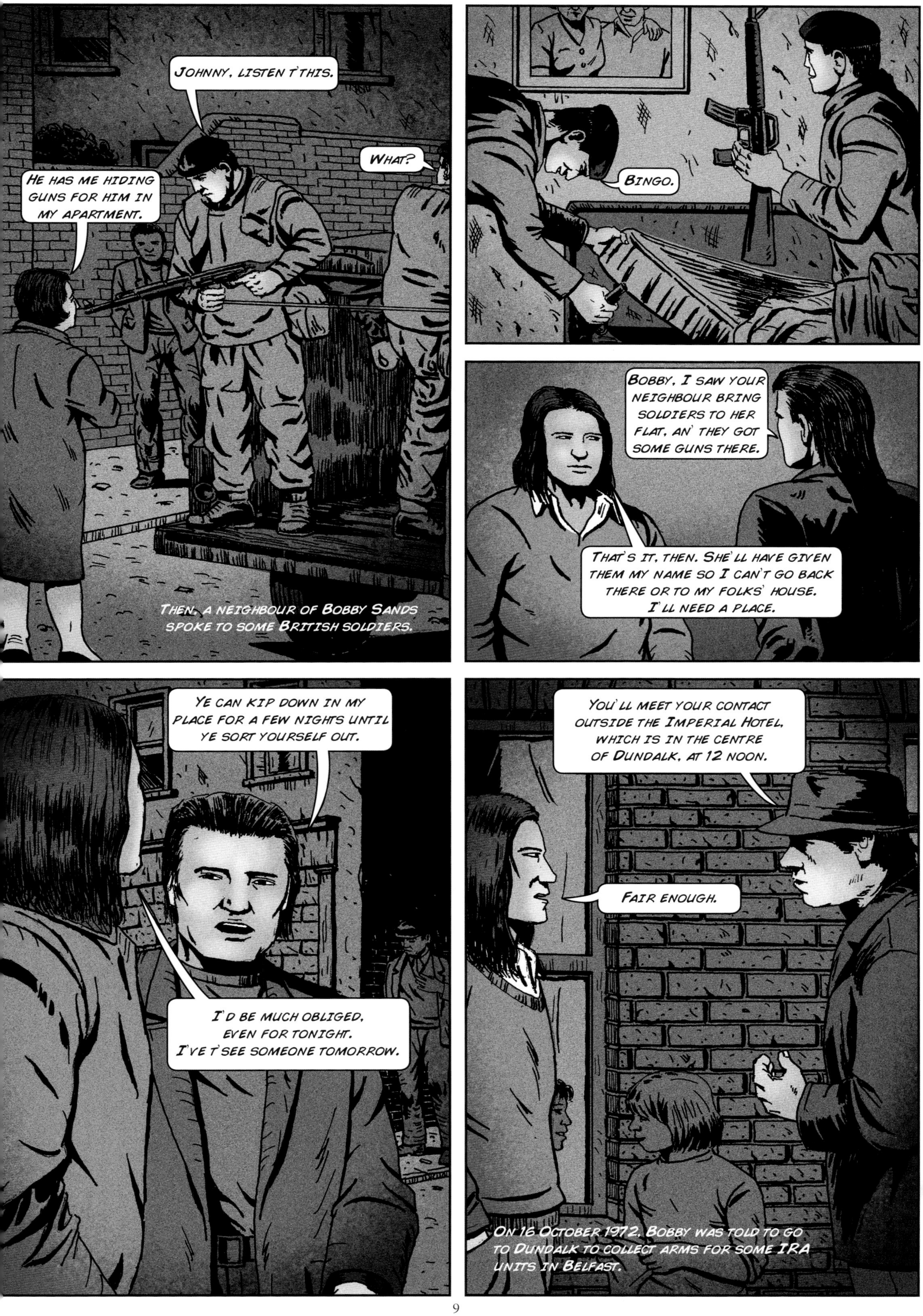
Johnny, listen t' this.
He has me hiding guns for him in my apartment.
What?
Then, a neighbour of Bobby Sands spoke to some British soldiers.
Bingo.
Bobby, I saw your neighbour bring soldiers to her flat, an' they got some guns there.
That's it, then. She'll have given them my name so I can't go back there or to my folks' house. I'll need a place.
Ye can kip down in my place for a few nights until ye sort yourself out.
I'd be much obliged, even for tonight. I've t' see someone tomorrow.
You'll meet your contact outside the Imperial Hotel, which is in the centre of Dundalk, at 12 noon.
Fair enough.
On 16 October 1972, Bobby was told to go to Dundalk to collect arms for some IRA units in Belfast.

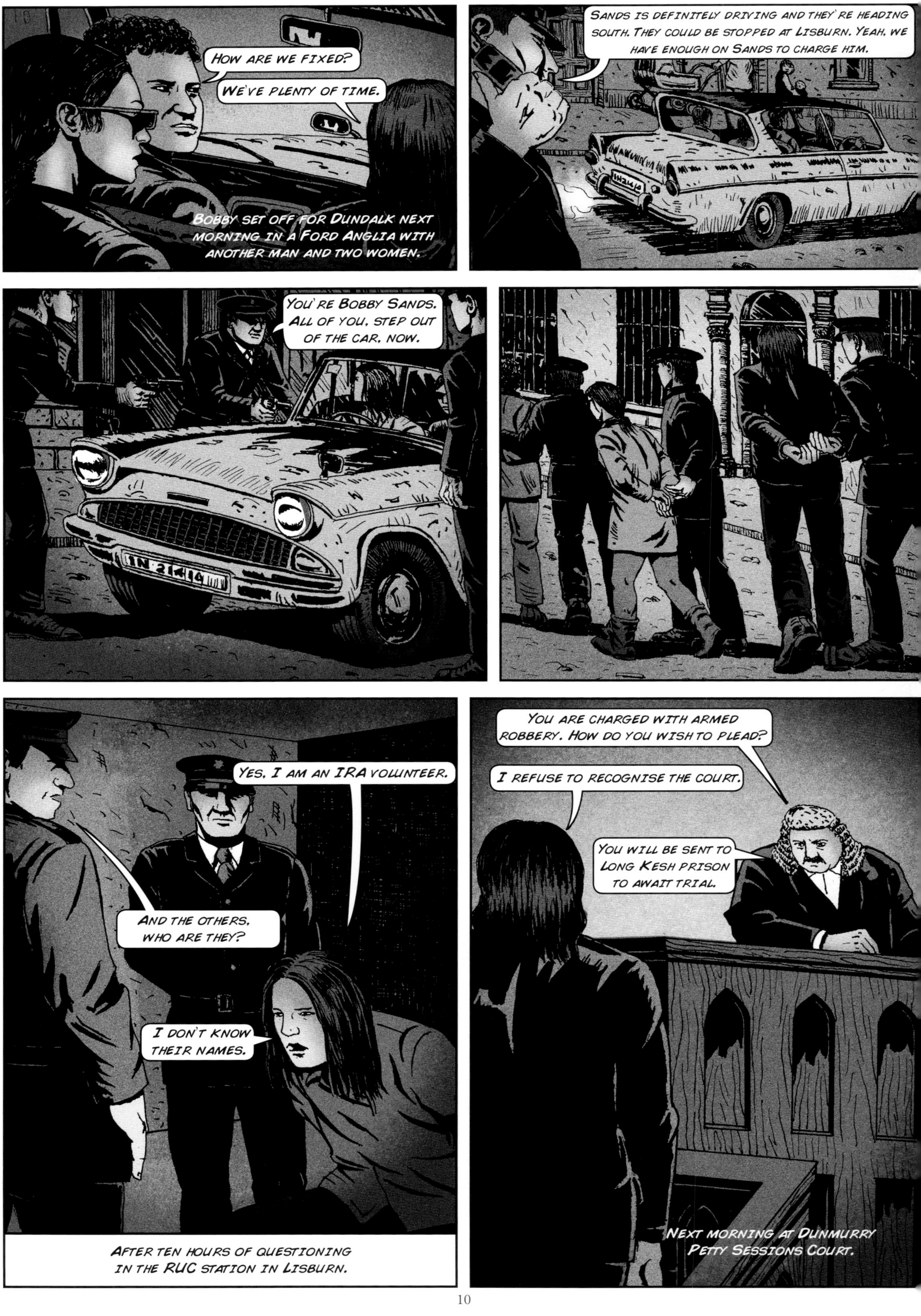
How are we fixed?
We've plenty of time.
Bobby set off for Dundalk next morning in a Ford Anglia with another man and two women.
Sands is definitely driving and they're heading south. They could be stopped at Lisburn. Yeah, we have enough on Sands to charge him.
You're Bobby Sands. All of you, step out of the car, now.
Yes, I am an IRA volunteer.
And the others, who are they?
I don't know their names.
After ten hours of questioning in the RUC station in Lisburn.
You are charged with armed robbery. How do you wish to plead?
I refuse to recognise the court.
You will be sent to Long Kesh prison to await trial.
Next morning at Dunmurry Petty Sessions Court.

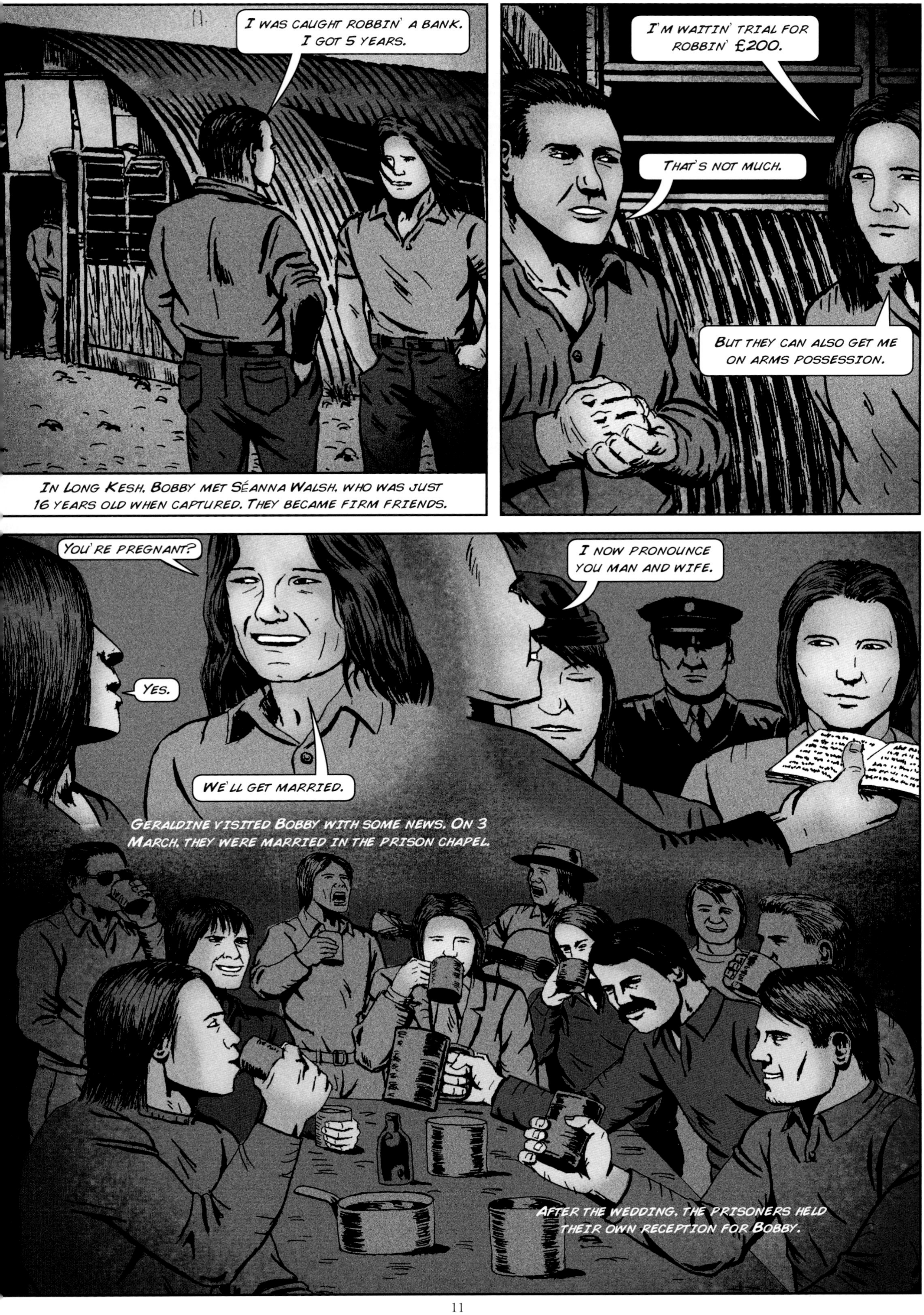
I WAS CAUGHT ROBBIN' A BANK. I GOT 5 YEARS.
IN LONG KESH, BOBBY MET SÉANNA WALSH, WHO WAS JUST 16 YEARS OLD WHEN CAPTURED. THEY BECAME FIRM FRIENDS.
I'M WAITIN' TRIAL FOR ROBBIN' £200.
THAT'S NOT MUCH.
BUT THEY CAN ALSO GET ME ON ARMS POSSESSION.
YOU'RE PREGNANT?
YES.
WE'LL GET MARRIED.
I NOW PRONOUNCE YOU MAN AND WIFE.
GERALDINE VISITED BOBBY WITH SOME NEWS. ON 3 MARCH, THEY WERE MARRIED IN THE PRISON CHAPEL.
AFTER THE WEDDING, THE PRISONERS HELD THEIR OWN RECEPTION FOR BOBBY.

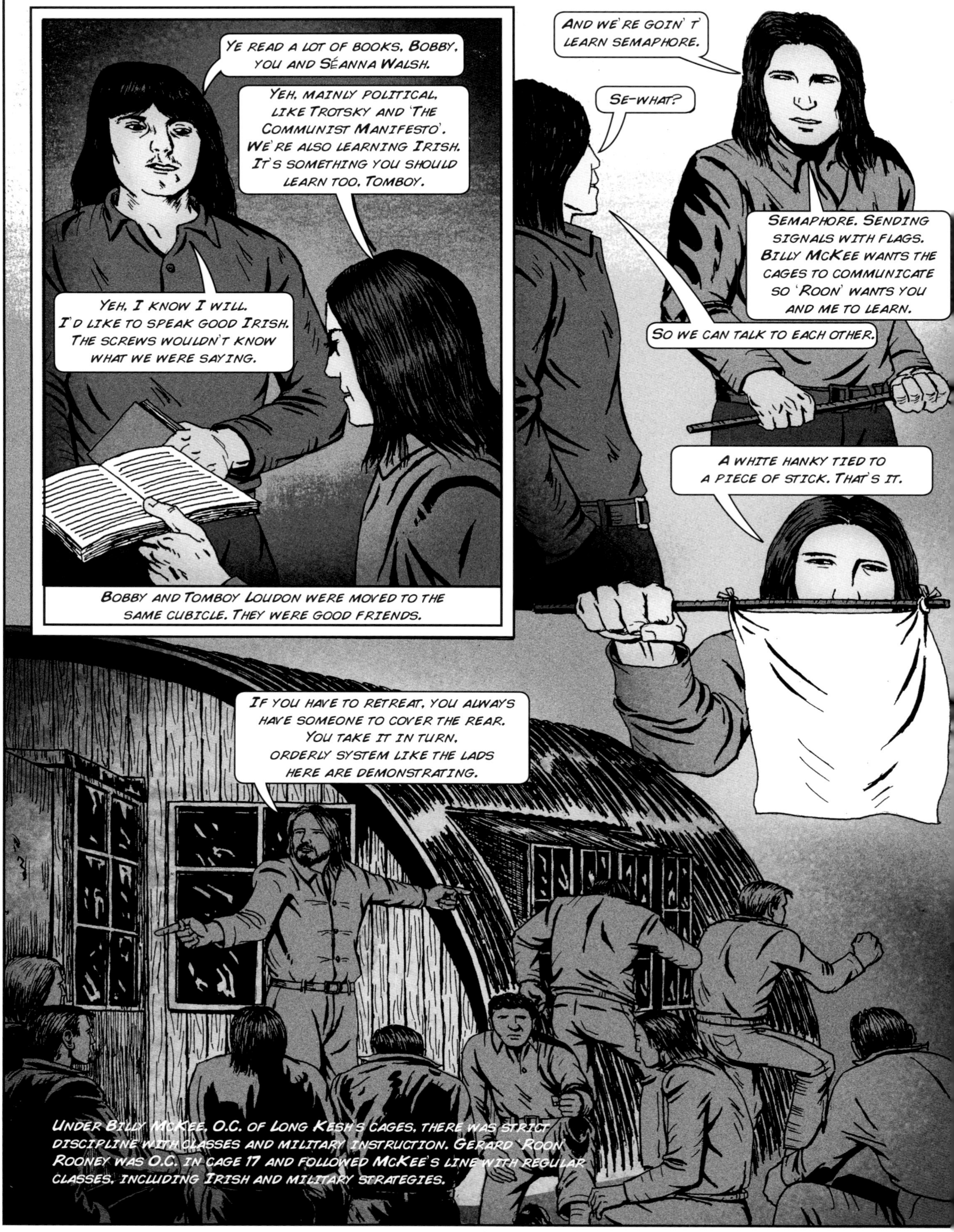
YE READ A LOT OF BOOKS, BOBBY, YOU AND SÉANNA WALSH.
YEH, MAINLY POLITICAL, LIKE TROTSKY AND 'THE COMMUNIST MANIFESTO'. WE'RE ALSO LEARNING IRISH. IT'S SOMETHING YOU SHOULD LEARN TOO, TOMBOY.
YEH, I KNOW I WILL. I'D LIKE TO SPEAK GOOD IRISH. THE SCREWS WOULDN'T KNOW WHAT WE WERE SAYING.
BOBBY AND TOMBOY LOUDON WERE MOVED TO THE SAME CUBICLE. THEY WERE GOOD FRIENDS.
AND WE'RE GOIN' T' LEARN SEMAPHORE.
SE-WHAT?
SEMAPHORE. SENDING SIGNALS WITH FLAGS. BILLY MCKEE WANTS THE CAGES TO COMMUNICATE SO 'ROON' WANTS YOU AND ME TO LEARN.
SO WE CAN TALK TO EACH OTHER.
A WHITE HANKY TIED TO A PIECE OF STICK. THAT'S IT.
IF YOU HAVE TO RETREAT, YOU ALWAYS HAVE SOMEONE TO COVER THE REAR. YOU TAKE IT IN TURN, ORDERLY SYSTEM LIKE THE LADS HERE ARE DEMONSTRATING.
UNDER BILLY MCKEE, O.C. OF LONG KESH'S CAGES, THERE WAS STRICT DISCIPLINE WITH CLASSES AND MILITARY INSTRUCTION. GERARD 'ROON' ROONEY WAS O.C. IN CAGE 17 AND FOLLOWED MCKEE'S LINE WITH REGULAR CLASSES, INCLUDING IRISH AND MILITARY STRATEGIES.

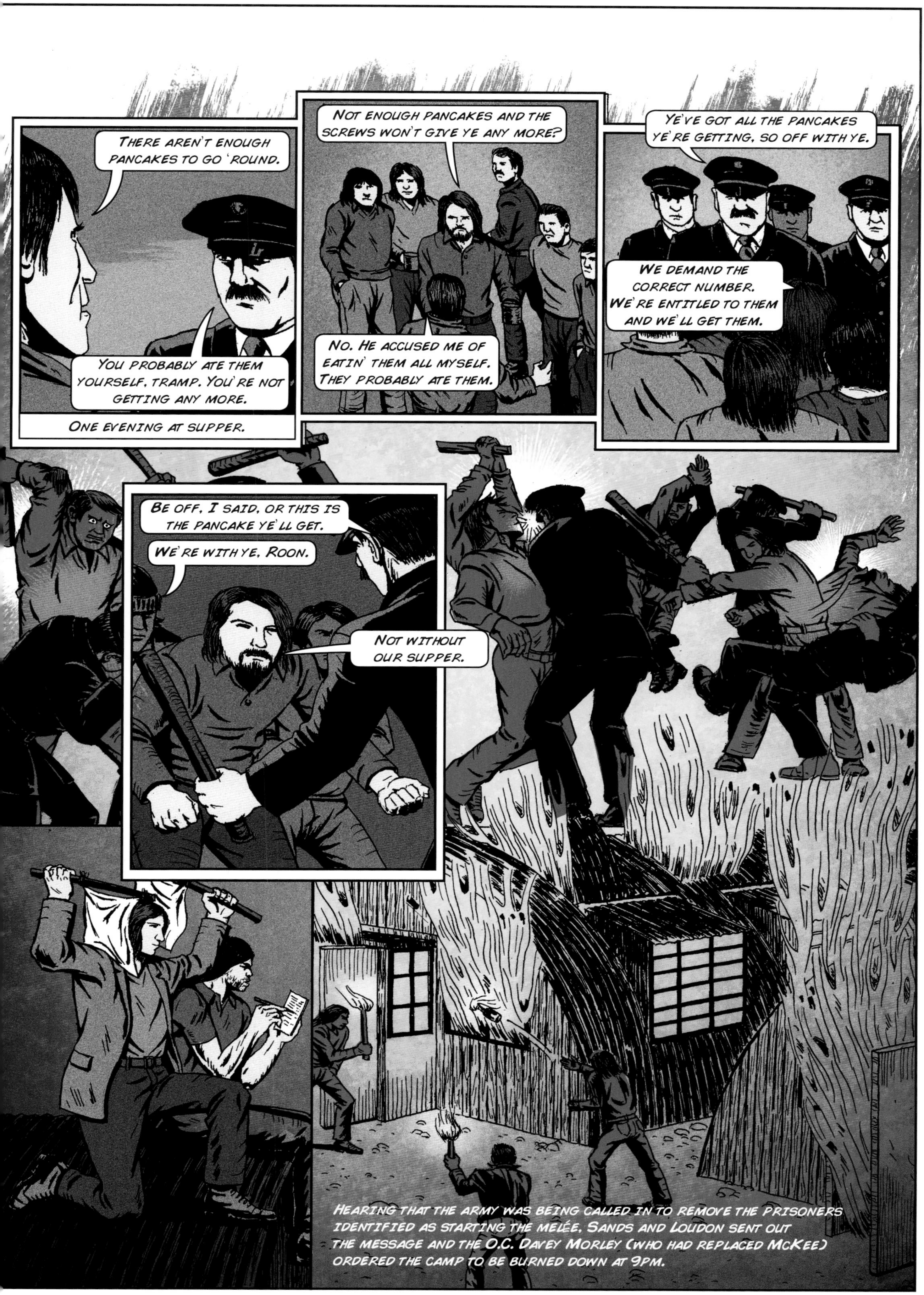

THERE AREN'T ENOUGH PANCAKES TO GO 'ROUND.
YOU PROBABLY ATE THEM YOURSELF, TRAMP. YOU'RE NOT GETTING ANY MORE.
ONE EVENING AT SUPPER.
NOT ENOUGH PANCAKES AND THE SCREWS WON'T GIVE YE ANY MORE?
NO. HE ACCUSED ME OF EATIN' THEM ALL MYSELF. THEY PROBABLY ATE THEM.
YE'VE GOT ALL THE PANCAKES YE'RE GETTING, SO OFF WITH YE.
WE DEMAND THE CORRECT NUMBER. WE'RE ENTITLED TO THEM AND WE'LL GET THEM.
BE OFF, I SAID, OR THIS IS THE PANCAKE YE'LL GET.
WE'RE WITH YE, ROON.
NOT WITHOUT OUR SUPPER.
HEARING THAT THE ARMY WAS BEING CALLED IN TO REMOVE THE PRISONERS IDENTIFIED AS STARTING THE MELÉE, SANDS AND LOUDON SENT OUT THE MESSAGE AND THE O.C. DAVEY MORLEY (WHO HAD REPLACED MCKEE) ORDERED THE CAMP TO BE BURNED DOWN AT 9PM.

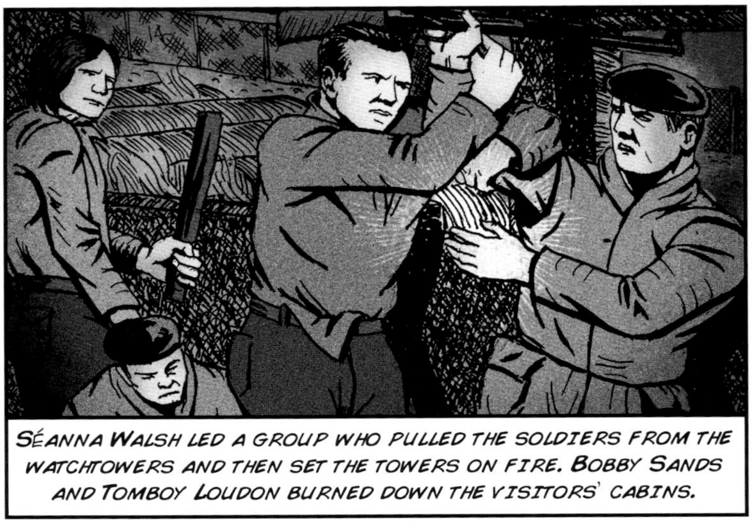
SÉANNA WALSH LED A GROUP WHO PULLED THE SOLDIERS FROM THE WATCHTOWERS AND THEN SET THE TOWERS ON FIRE. BOBBY SANDS AND TOMBOY LOUDON BURNED DOWN THE VISITORS' CABINS.

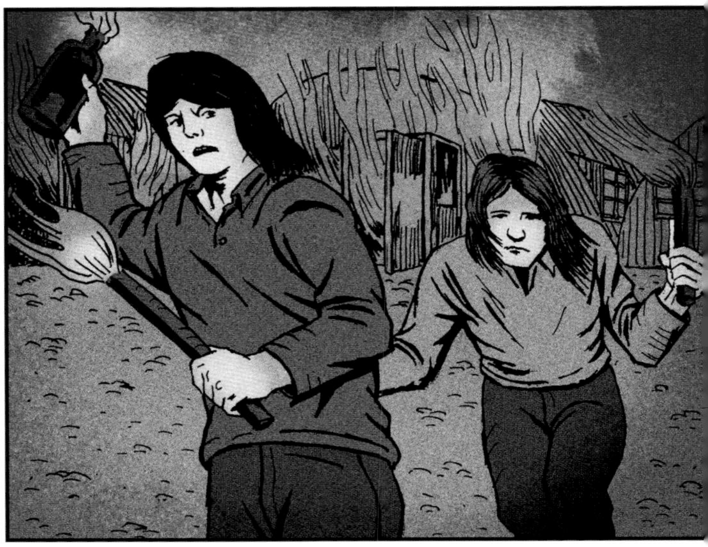

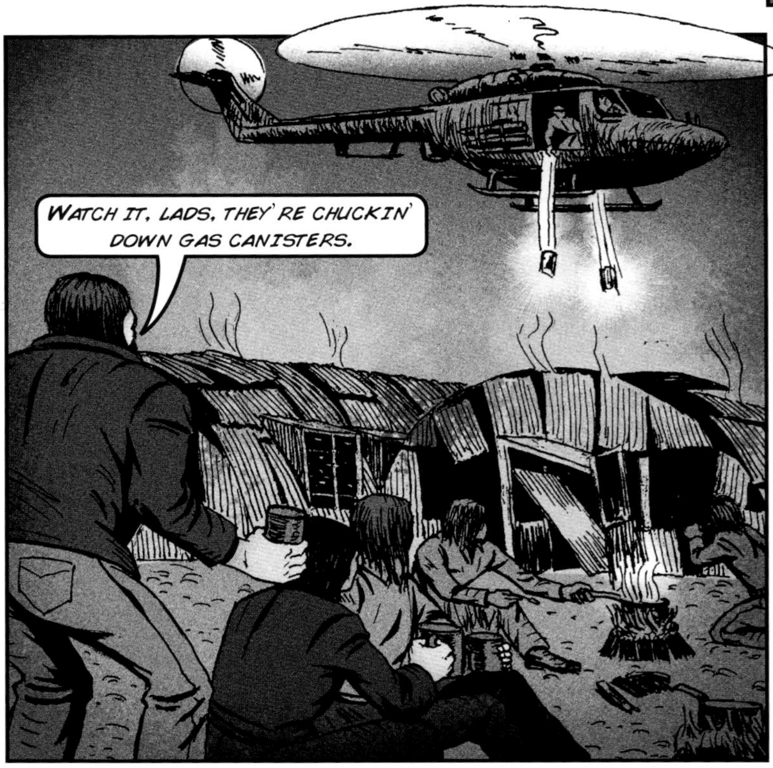
WATCH IT, LADS, THEY'RE CHUCKIN' DOWN GAS CANISTERS.

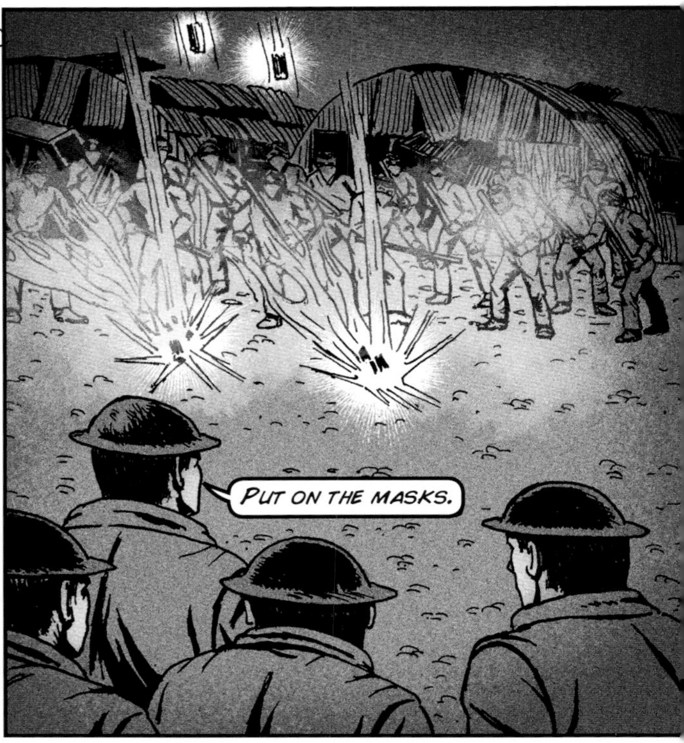
PUT ON THE MASKS.

THE PRISONERS WERE NOW OUT IN THE OPEN AND LIT FIRES OVER WHICH THEY HEATED TINNED FOOD THEY HAD TAKEN FROM THE PRISON TUCK SHOP, ALL THE TIME TRYING TO DODGE THE GAS CANISTERS FROM THE HELICOPTERS. AT DAWN, THE BRITISH ARMY ARRIVED.

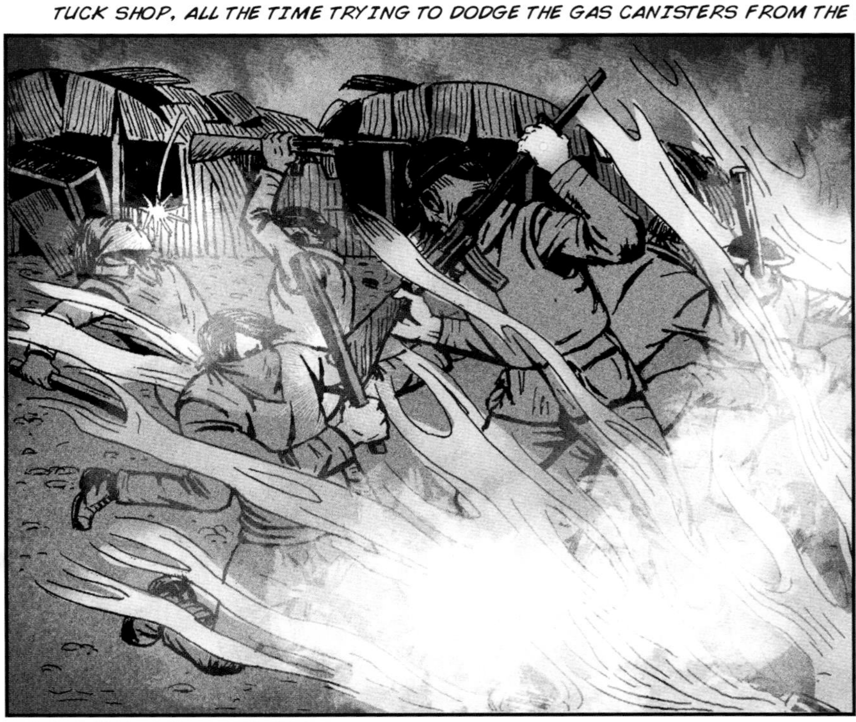

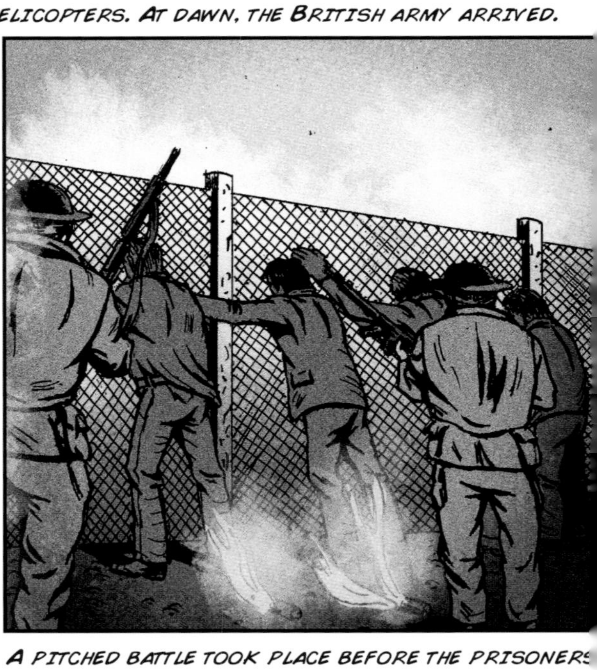

A PITCHED BATTLE TOOK PLACE BEFORE THE PRISONERS WERE FINALLY OVERWHELMED BY THE WELL-PREPARED SOLDIERS AND THE GAS.

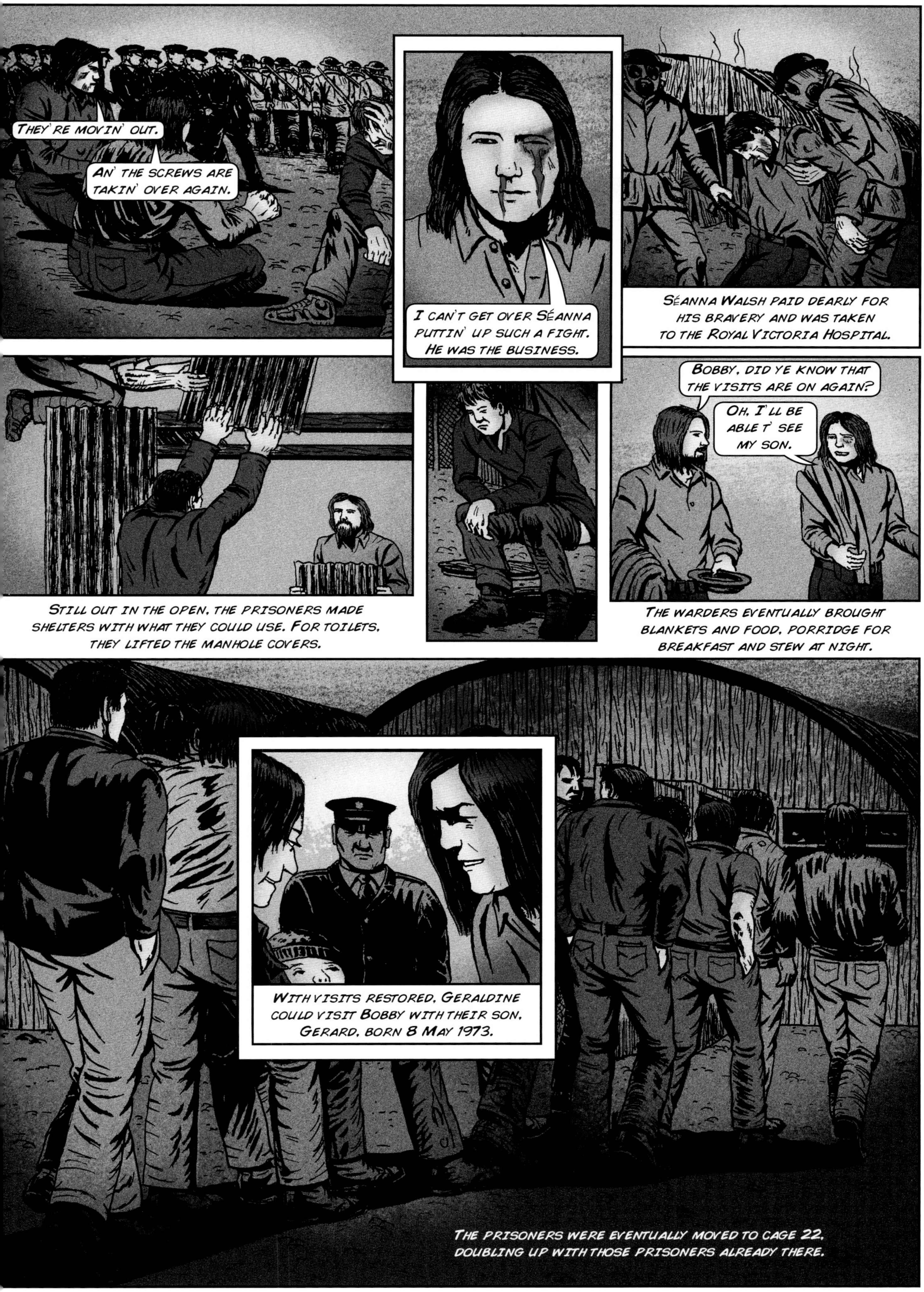
They're movin' out.
An' the screws are takin' over again.
I can't get over Séanna puttin' up such a fight. He was the business.
Séanna Walsh paid dearly for his bravery and was taken to the Royal Victoria Hospital.
Still out in the open, the prisoners made shelters with what they could use. For toilets, they lifted the manhole covers.
Bobby, did ye know that the visits are on again?
Oh, I'll be able t' see my son.
The warders eventually brought blankets and food, porridge for breakfast and stew at night.
With visits restored, Geraldine could visit Bobby with their son, Gerard, born 8 May 1973.
The prisoners were eventually moved to cage 22, doubling up with those prisoners already there.

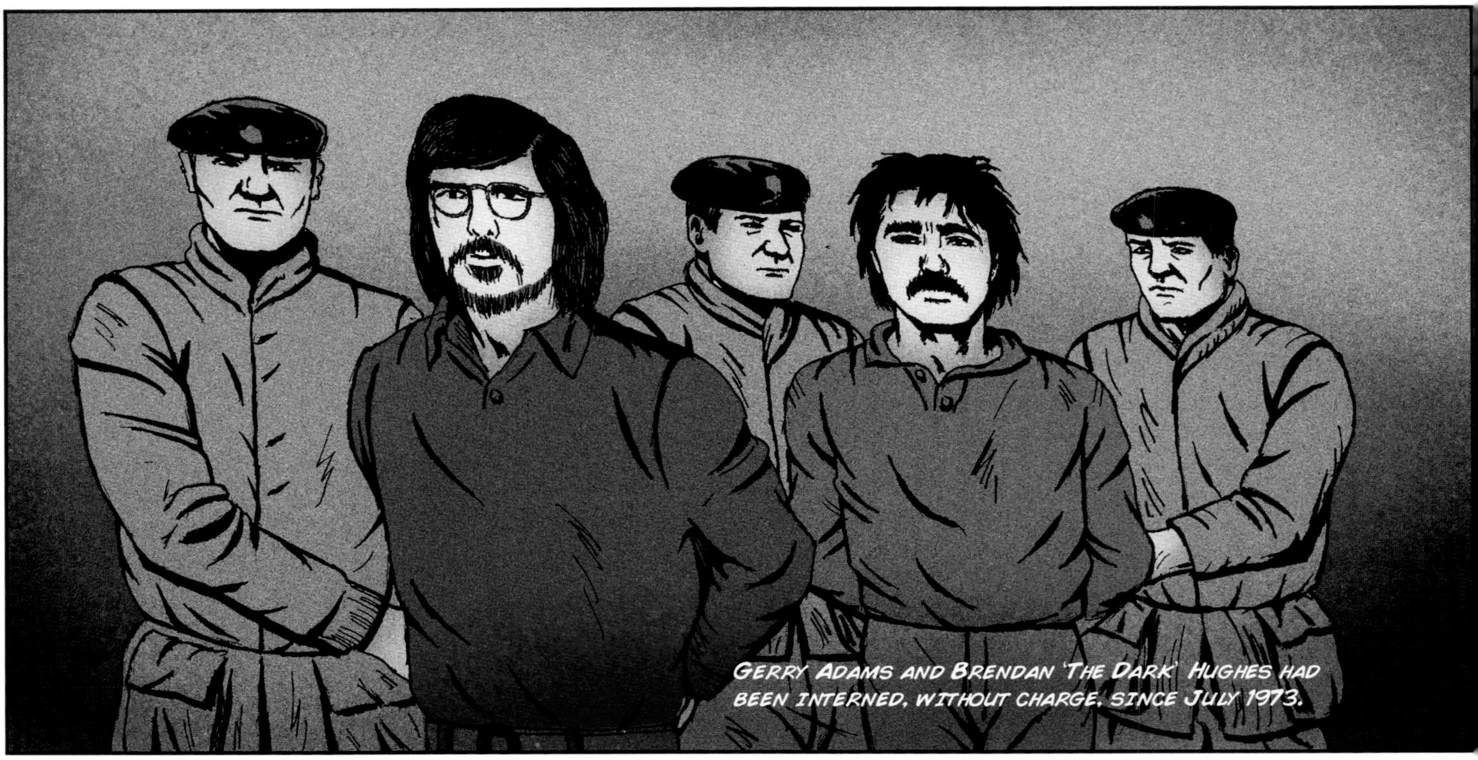
GERRY ADAMS AND BRENDAN 'THE DARK' HUGHES HAD BEEN INTERNED, WITHOUT CHARGE, SINCE JULY 1973.

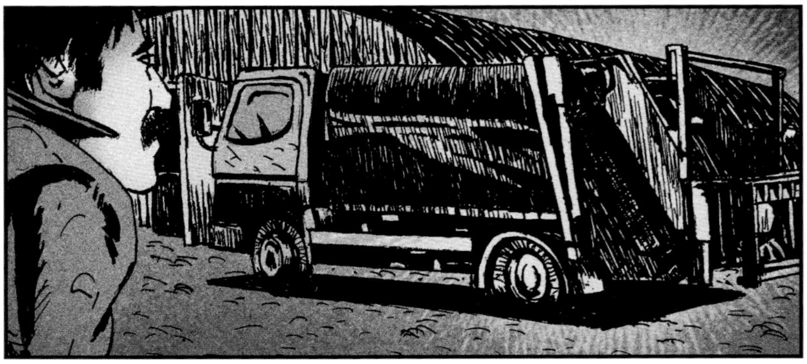

IN DECEMBER, BRENDAN HUGHES ESCAPED IN THE BACK OF A REFUSE DISPOSAL TRUCK.

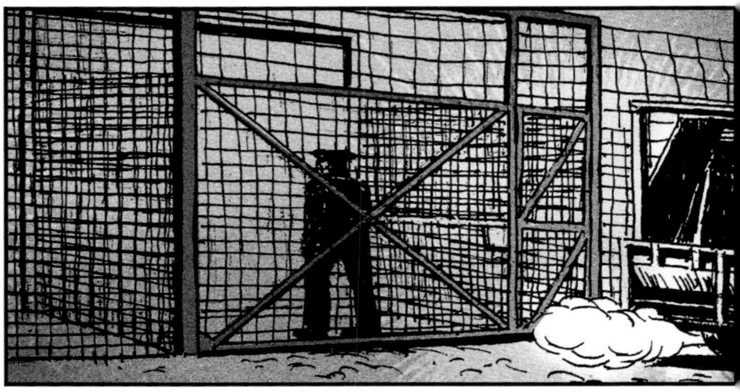

ADAMS WAS CAUGHT TRYING TO ESCAPE FOR THE SECOND TIME. HE GOT A SENTENCE OF EIGHTEEN MONTHS. HE WAS SENT TO A CAGE AND VERY SOON GOT TO KNOW BOBBY SANDS.

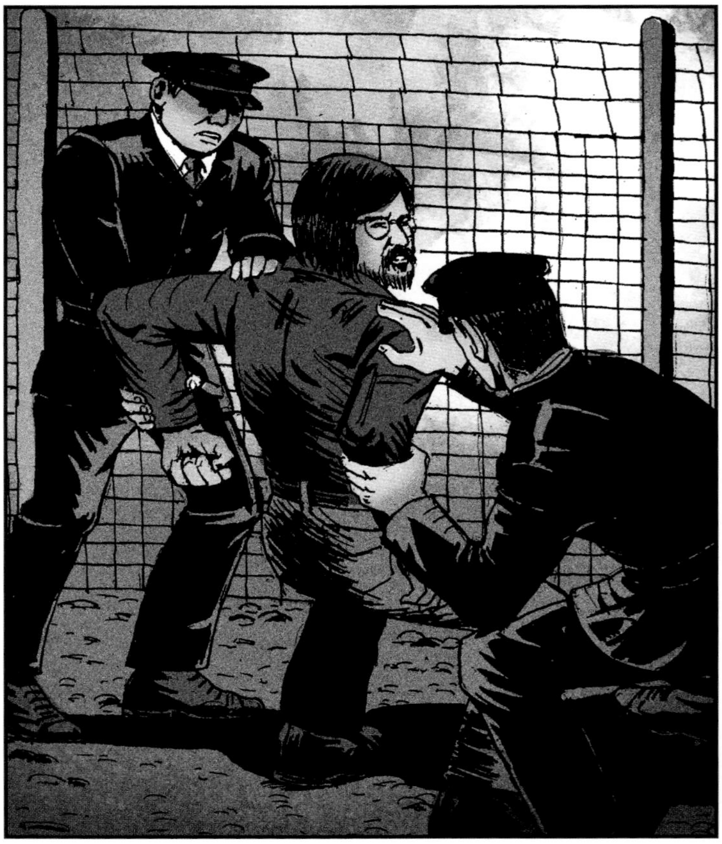

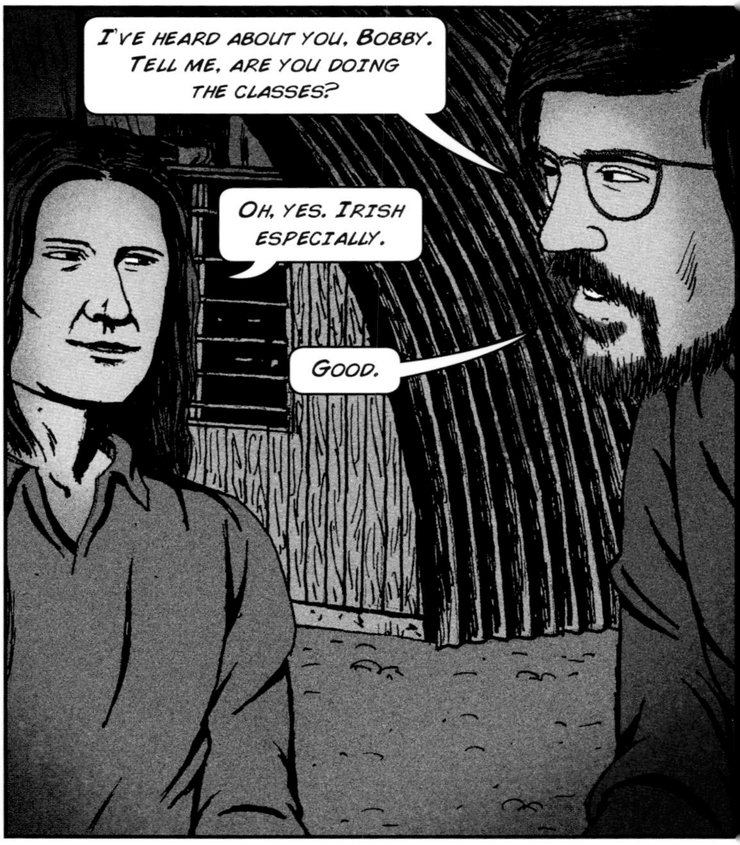
I'VE HEARD ABOUT YOU, BOBBY. TELL ME, ARE YOU DOING THE CLASSES?
OH, YES. IRISH ESPECIALLY.
GOOD.

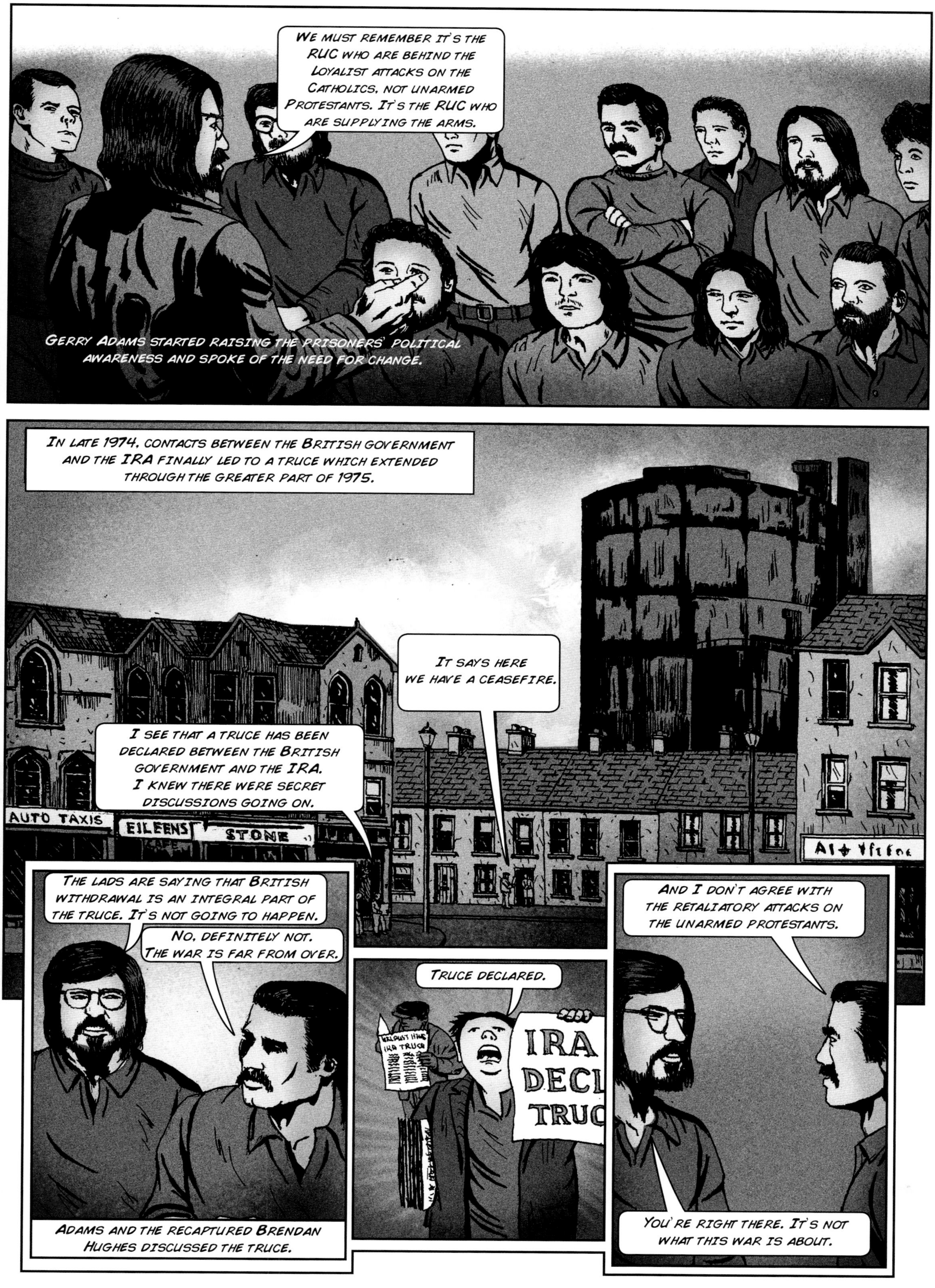

We must remember it's the RUC who are behind the Loyalist attacks on the Catholics, not unarmed Protestants. It's the RUC who are supplying the arms.
Gerry Adams started raising the prisoners' political awareness and spoke of the need for change.
In late 1974, contacts between the British government and the IRA finally led to a truce which extended through the greater part of 1975.
I see that a truce has been declared between the British government and the IRA. I knew there were secret discussions going on.
It says here we have a ceasefire.
AUTO TAXIS
EILEENS
STONE
The lads are saying that British withdrawal is an integral part of the truce. It's not going to happen.
No, definitely not. The war is far from over.
Adams and the recaptured Brendan Hughes discussed the truce.
Truce declared.
IRA
DECL
TRUC
And I don't agree with the retaliatory attacks on the unarmed Protestants.
You're right there. It's not what this war is about.

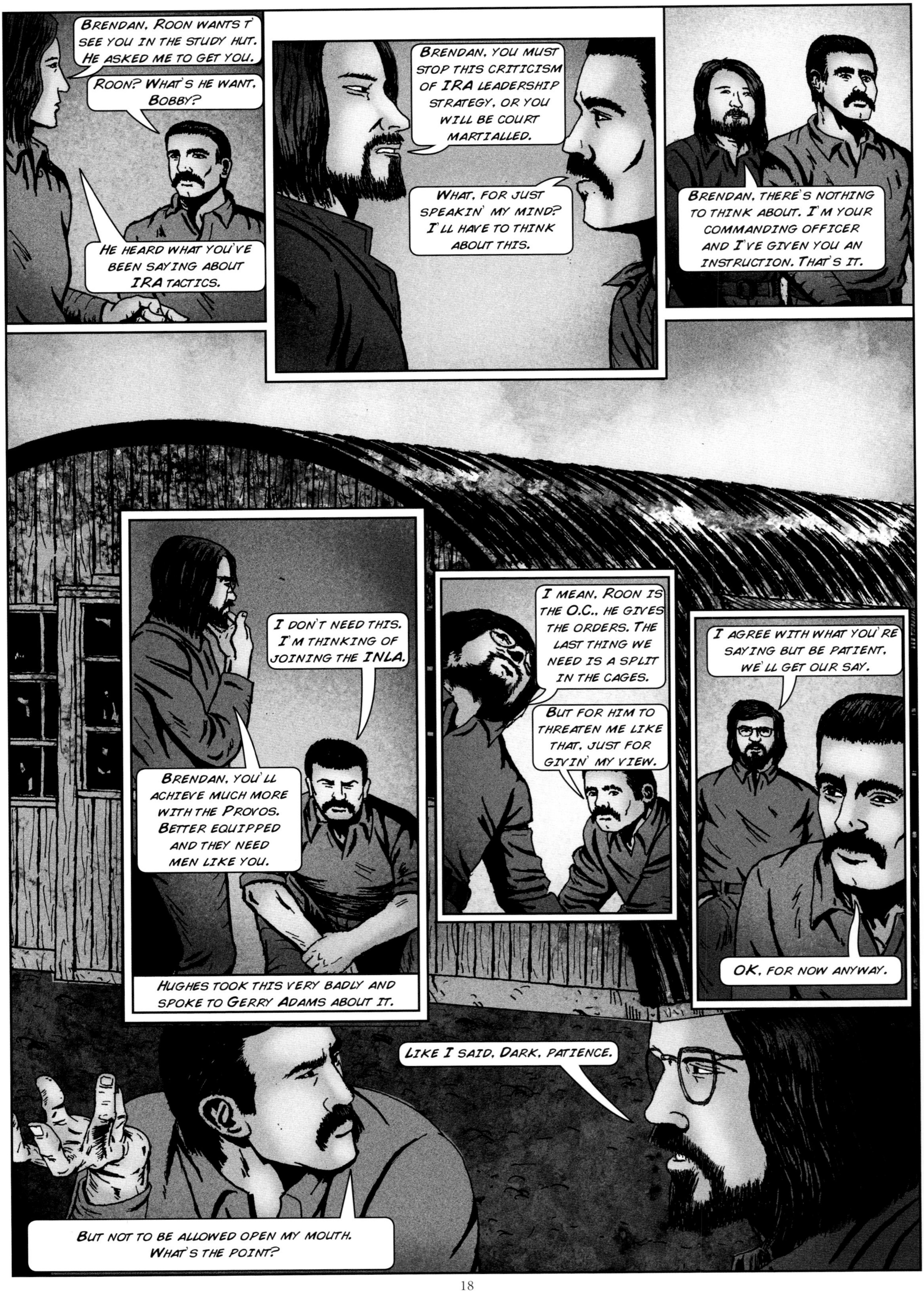
BRENDAN, ROON WANTS T' SEE YOU IN THE STUDY HUT. HE ASKED ME TO GET YOU.
ROON? WHAT'S HE WANT, BOBBY?
HE HEARD WHAT YOU'VE BEEN SAYING ABOUT IRA TACTICS.
BRENDAN, YOU MUST STOP THIS CRITICISM OF IRA LEADERSHIP STRATEGY, OR YOU WILL BE COURT MARTIALLED.
WHAT, FOR JUST SPEAKIN' MY MIND? I'LL HAVE TO THINK ABOUT THIS.
BRENDAN, THERE'S NOTHING TO THINK ABOUT. I'M YOUR COMMANDING OFFICER AND I'VE GIVEN YOU AN INSTRUCTION. THAT'S IT.
I DON'T NEED THIS. I'M THINKING OF JOINING THE INLA.
BRENDAN, YOU'LL ACHIEVE MUCH MORE WITH THE PROVOS. BETTER EQUIPPED AND THEY NEED MEN LIKE YOU.
HUGHES TOOK THIS VERY BADLY AND SPOKE TO GERRY ADAMS ABOUT IT.
I MEAN, ROON IS THE O.C., HE GIVES THE ORDERS. THE LAST THING WE NEED IS A SPLIT IN THE CAGES.
BUT FOR HIM TO THREATEN ME LIKE THAT, JUST FOR GIVIN' MY VIEW.
I AGREE WITH WHAT YOU'RE SAYING BUT BE PATIENT, WE'LL GET OUR SAY.
OK, FOR NOW ANYWAY.
LIKE I SAID, DARK, PATIENCE.
BUT NOT TO BE ALLOWED OPEN MY MOUTH. WHAT'S THE POINT?

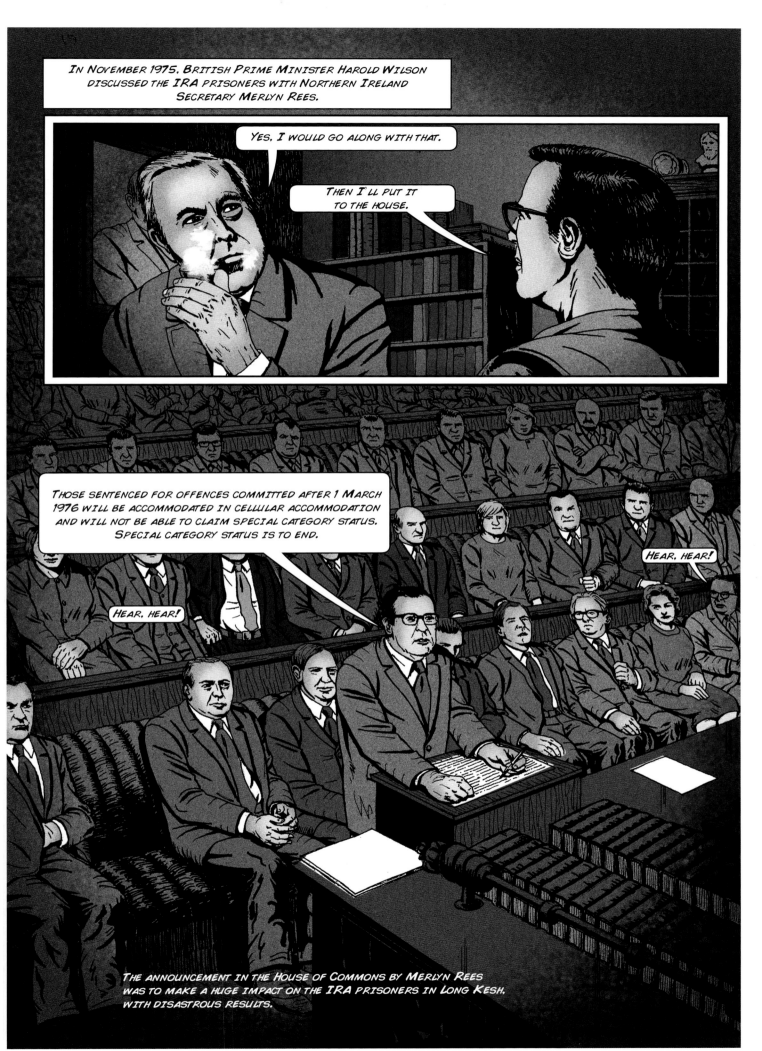

IN NOVEMBER 1975, BRITISH PRIME MINISTER HAROLD WILSON DISCUSSED THE IRA PRISONERS WITH NORTHERN IRELAND SECRETARY MERLYN REES.

YES, I WOULD GO ALONG WITH THAT.

THEN I'LL PUT IT TO THE HOUSE.

THOSE SENTENCED FOR OFFENCES COMMITTED AFTER 1 MARCH 1976 WILL BE ACCOMMODATED IN CELLULAR ACCOMMODATION AND WILL NOT BE ABLE TO CLAIM SPECIAL CATEGORY STATUS. SPECIAL CATEGORY STATUS IS TO END.

HEAR, HEAR!

HEAR, HEAR!

THE ANNOUNCEMENT IN THE HOUSE OF COMMONS BY MERLYN REES WAS TO MAKE A HUGE IMPACT ON THE IRA PRISONERS IN LONG KESH, WITH DISASTROUS RESULTS.

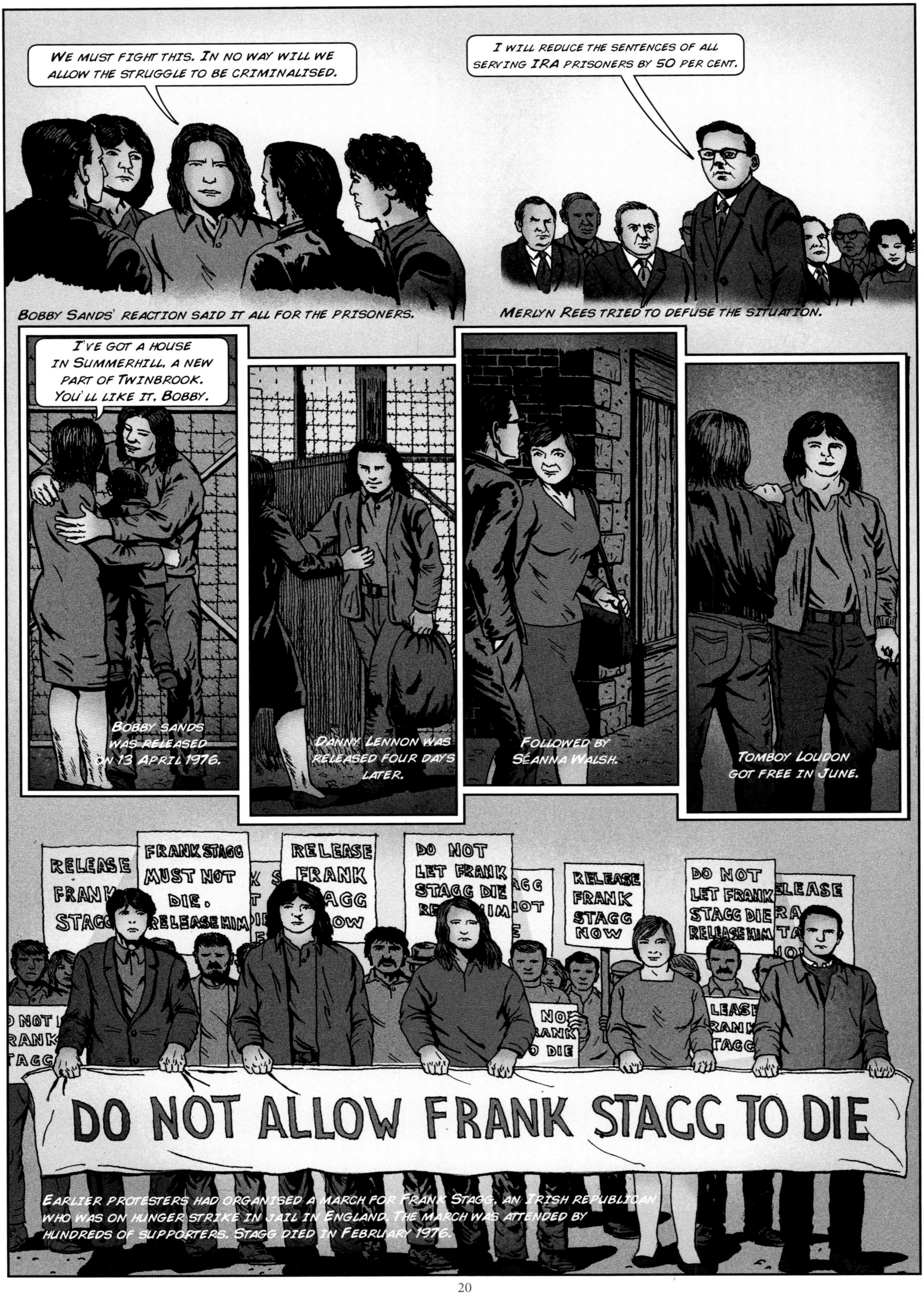
WE MUST FIGHT THIS. IN NO WAY WILL WE ALLOW THE STRUGGLE TO BE CRIMINALISED.
BOBBY SANDS' REACTION SAID IT ALL FOR THE PRISONERS.
I WILL REDUCE THE SENTENCES OF ALL SERVING IRA PRISONERS BY 50 PER CENT.
MERLYN REES TRIED TO DEFUSE THE SITUATION.
I'VE GOT A HOUSE IN SUMMERHILL, A NEW PART OF TWINBROOK. YOU'LL LIKE IT, BOBBY.
BOBBY SANDS WAS RELEASED ON 13 APRIL 1976.
DANNY LENNON WAS RELEASED FOUR DAYS LATER.
FOLLOWED BY SÉANNA WALSH.
TOMBOY LOUDON GOT FREE IN JUNE.
RELEASE FRANK STAGG
FRANK STAGG MUST NOT DIE. RELEASE HIM
RELEASE FRANK STAGG NOW
DO NOT LET FRANK STAGG DIE RELEASE HIM
RELEASE FRANK STAGG NOW
DO NOT LET FRANK STAGG DIE RELEASE HIM
DO NOT ALLOW FRANK STAGG TO DIE
EARLIER PROTESTERS HAD ORGANISED A MARCH FOR FRANK STAGG, AN IRISH REPUBLICAN WHO WAS ON HUNGER STRIKE IN JAIL IN ENGLAND. THE MARCH WAS ATTENDED BY HUNDREDS OF SUPPORTERS. STAGG DIED IN FEBRUARY 1976.

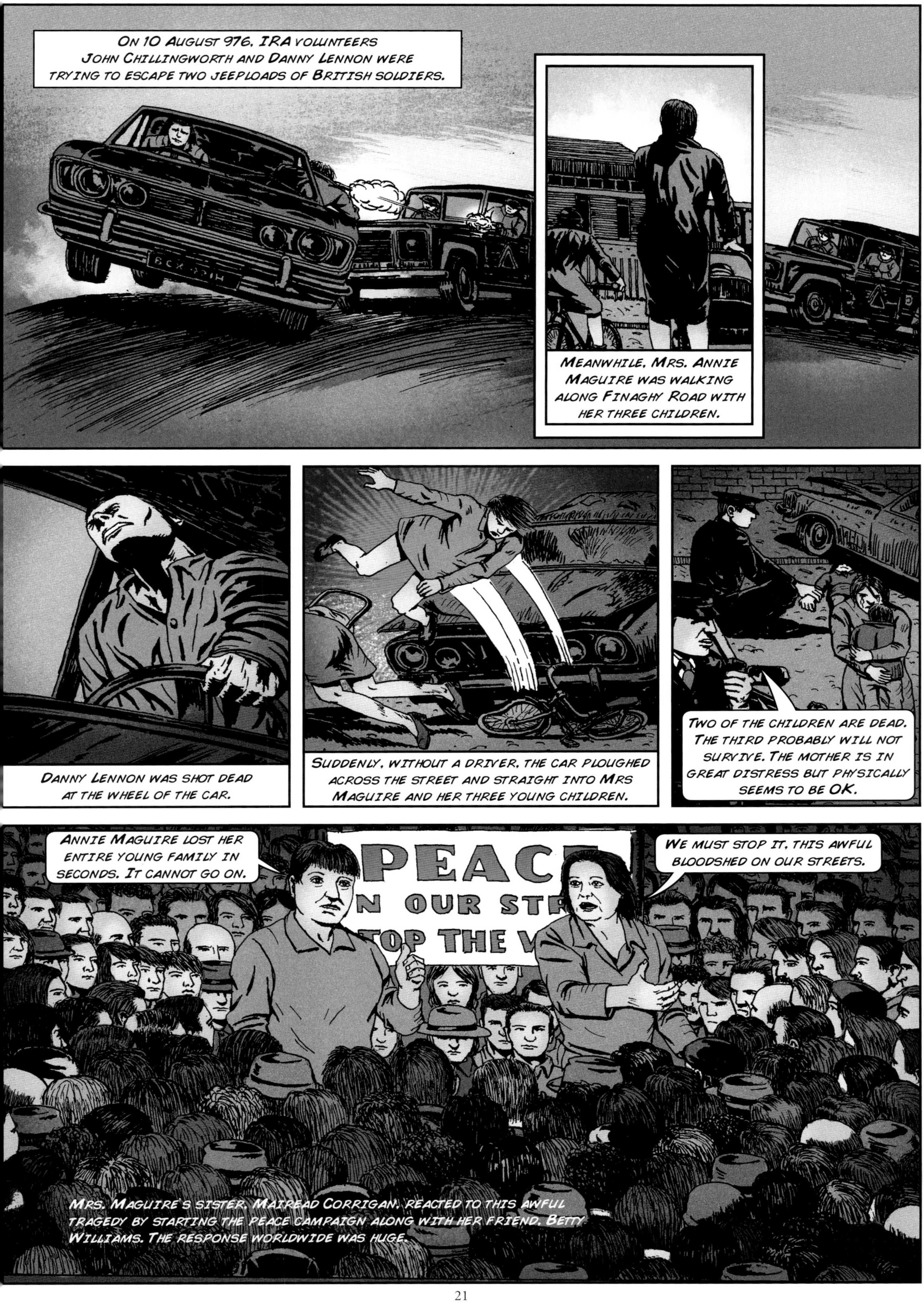
ON 10 AUGUST 976, IRA VOLUNTEERS JOHN CHILLINGWORTH AND DANNY LENNON WERE TRYING TO ESCAPE TWO JEEPLOADS OF BRITISH SOLDIERS.
MEANWHILE, MRS. ANNIE MAGUIRE WAS WALKING ALONG FINAGHY ROAD WITH HER THREE CHILDREN.
DANNY LENNON WAS SHOT DEAD AT THE WHEEL OF THE CAR.
SUDDENLY, WITHOUT A DRIVER, THE CAR PLOUGHED ACROSS THE STREET AND STRAIGHT INTO MRS MAGUIRE AND HER THREE YOUNG CHILDREN.
TWO OF THE CHILDREN ARE DEAD. THE THIRD PROBABLY WILL NOT SURVIVE. THE MOTHER IS IN GREAT DISTRESS BUT PHYSICALLY SEEMS TO BE OK.
ANNIE MAGUIRE LOST HER ENTIRE YOUNG FAMILY IN SECONDS. IT CANNOT GO ON.
WE MUST STOP IT, THIS AWFUL BLOODSHED ON OUR STREETS.
MRS. MAGUIRE'S SISTER, MAIREAD CORRIGAN, REACTED TO THIS AWFUL TRAGEDY BY STARTING THE PEACE CAMPAIGN ALONG WITH HER FRIEND, BETTY WILLIAMS. THE RESPONSE WORLDWIDE WAS HUGE.

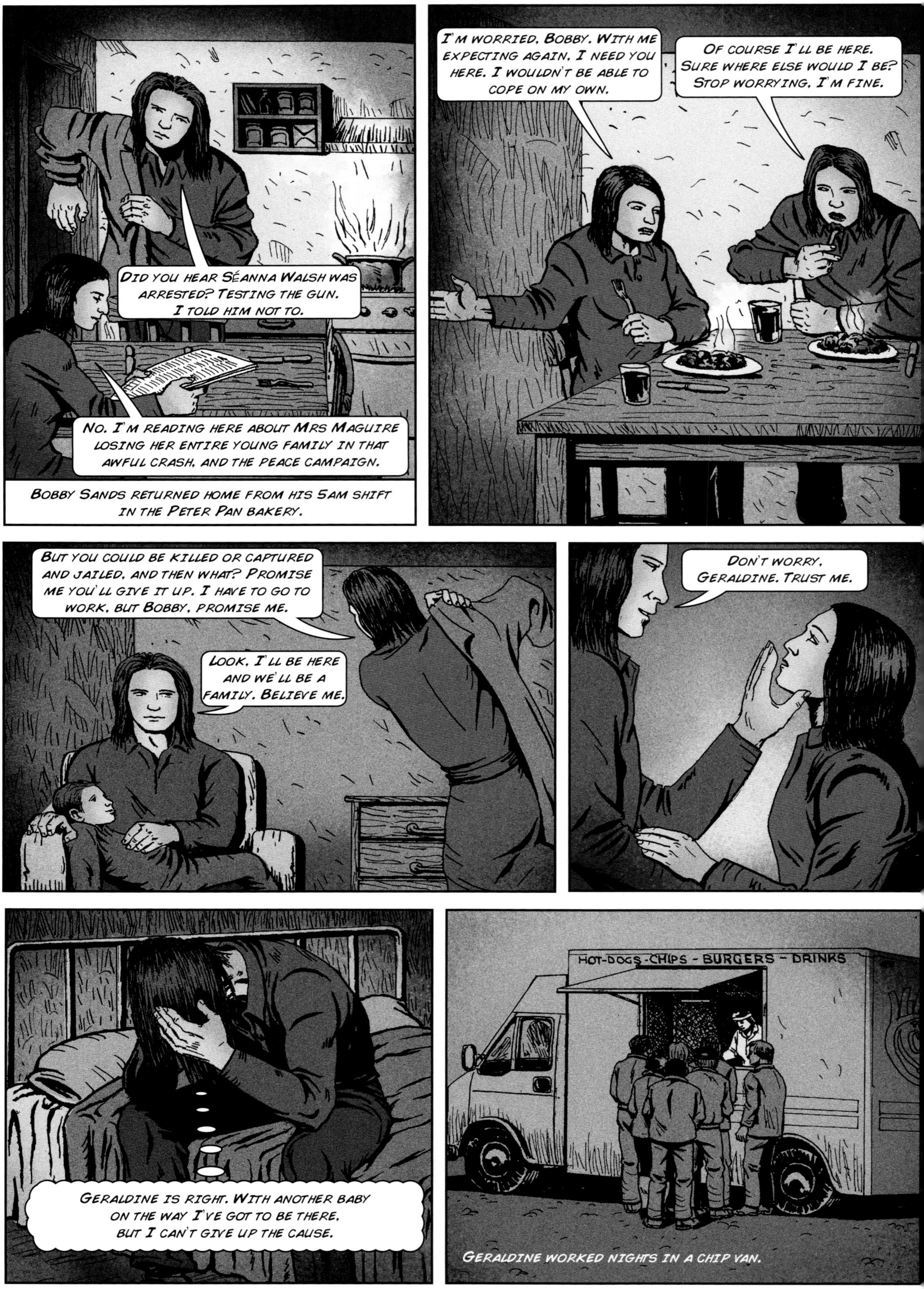
DID YOU HEAR SÉANNA WALSH WAS ARRESTED? TESTING THE GUN. I TOLD HIM NOT TO.
NO. I'M READING HERE ABOUT MRS MAGUIRE LOSING HER ENTIRE YOUNG FAMILY IN THAT AWFUL CRASH, AND THE PEACE CAMPAIGN.
BOBBY SANDS RETURNED HOME FROM HIS 5AM SHIFT IN THE PETER PAN BAKERY.
I'M WORRIED, BOBBY. WITH ME EXPECTING AGAIN, I NEED YOU HERE. I WOULDN'T BE ABLE TO COPE ON MY OWN.
OF COURSE I'LL BE HERE. SURE WHERE ELSE WOULD I BE? STOP WORRYING, I'M FINE.
BUT YOU COULD BE KILLED OR CAPTURED AND JAILED, AND THEN WHAT? PROMISE ME YOU'LL GIVE IT UP. I HAVE TO GO TO WORK, BUT BOBBY, PROMISE ME.
LOOK, I'LL BE HERE AND WE'LL BE A FAMILY. BELIEVE ME.
DON'T WORRY, GERALDINE. TRUST ME.
GERALDINE IS RIGHT. WITH ANOTHER BABY ON THE WAY I'VE GOT TO BE THERE. BUT I CAN'T GIVE UP THE CAUSE.
HOT-DOGS - CHIPS - BURGERS - DRINKS
GERALDINE WORKED NIGHTS IN A CHIP VAN.

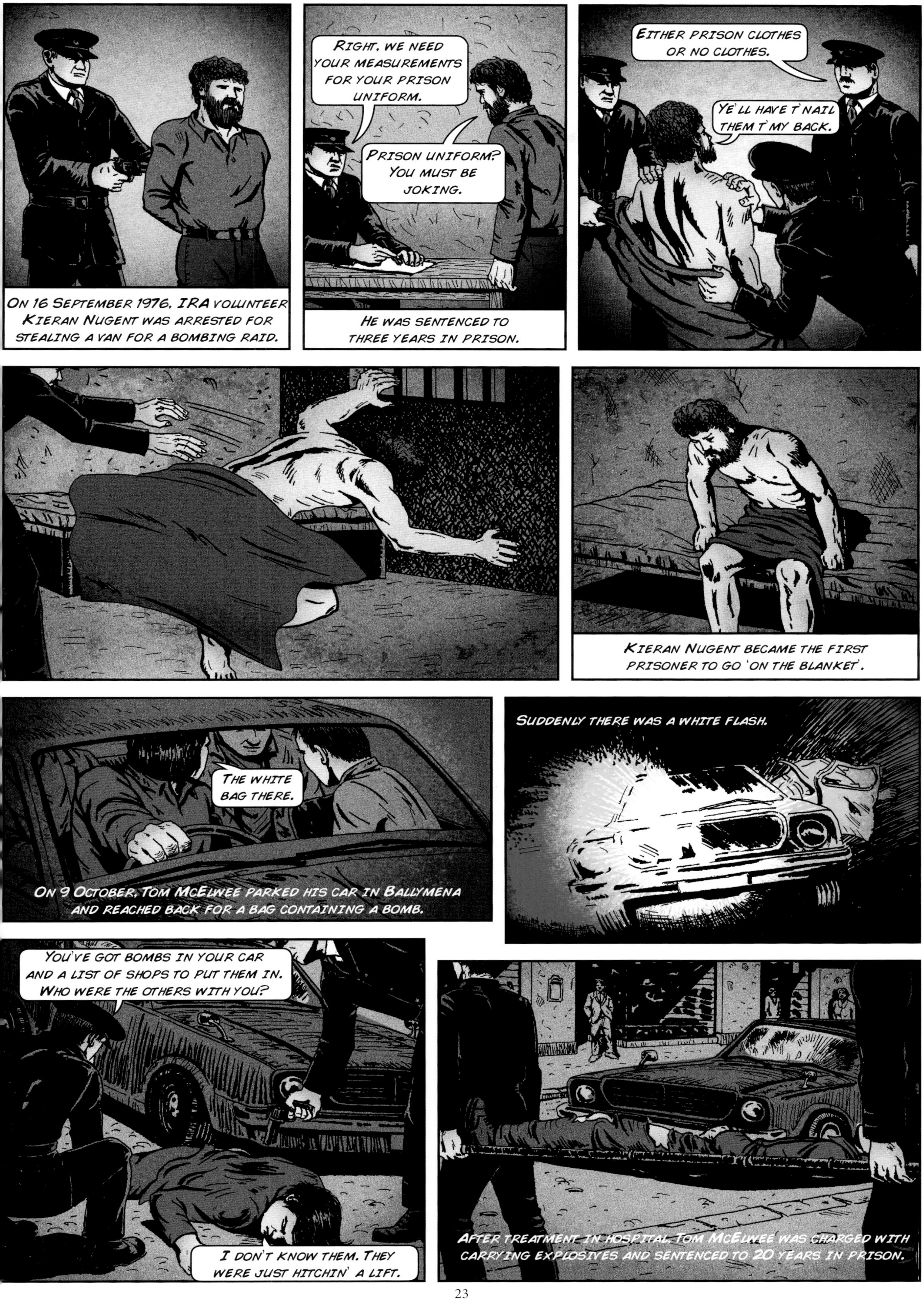
ON 16 SEPTEMBER 1976, IRA VOLUNTEER KIERAN NUGENT WAS ARRESTED FOR STEALING A VAN FOR A BOMBING RAID.
RIGHT, WE NEED YOUR MEASUREMENTS FOR YOUR PRISON UNIFORM.
PRISON UNIFORM? YOU MUST BE JOKING.
HE WAS SENTENCED TO THREE YEARS IN PRISON.
EITHER PRISON CLOTHES OR NO CLOTHES.
YE'LL HAVE T' NAIL THEM T' MY BACK.
KIERAN NUGENT BECAME THE FIRST PRISONER TO GO 'ON THE BLANKET'.
THE WHITE BAG THERE.
ON 9 OCTOBER, TOM MCELWEE PARKED HIS CAR IN BALLYMENA AND REACHED BACK FOR A BAG CONTAINING A BOMB.
SUDDENLY THERE WAS A WHITE FLASH.
YOU'VE GOT BOMBS IN YOUR CAR AND A LIST OF SHOPS TO PUT THEM IN. WHO WERE THE OTHERS WITH YOU?
I DON'T KNOW THEM. THEY WERE JUST HITCHIN' A LIFT.
AFTER TREATMENT IN HOSPITAL, TOM MCELWEE WAS CHARGED WITH CARRYING EXPLOSIVES AND SENTENCED TO 20 YEARS IN PRISON.

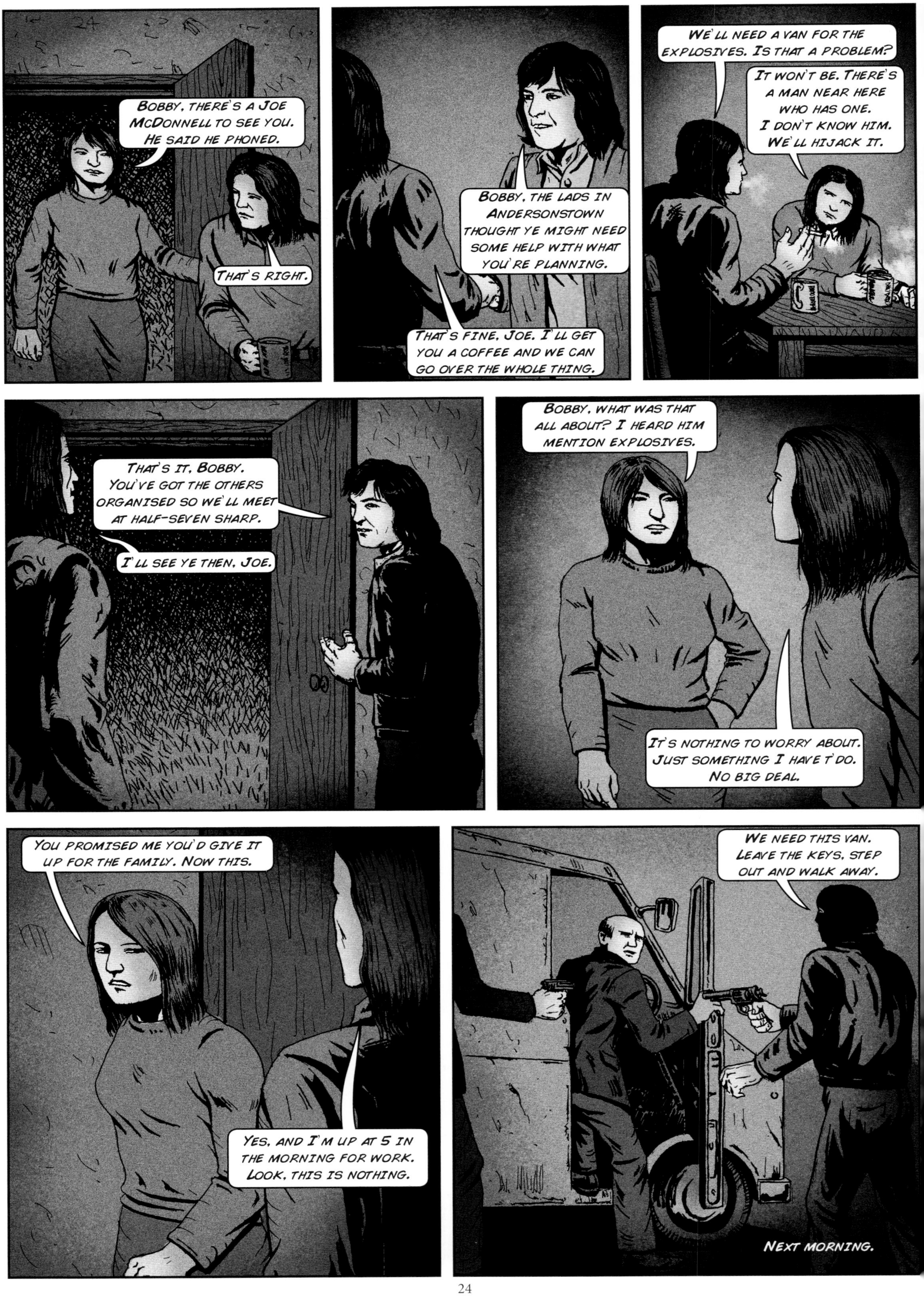
Bobby, there's a Joe McDonnell to see you. He said he phoned.
That's right.
Bobby, the lads in Andersonstown thought ye might need some help with what you're planning.
That's fine, Joe. I'll get you a coffee and we can go over the whole thing.
We'll need a van for the explosives. Is that a problem?
It won't be. There's a man near here who has one. I don't know him. We'll hijack it.
That's it, Bobby. You've got the others organised so we'll meet at half-seven sharp.
I'll see ye then, Joe.
Bobby, what was that all about? I heard him mention explosives.
It's nothing to worry about. Just something I have t' do. No big deal.
You promised me you'd give it up for the family. Now this.
Yes, and I'm up at 5 in the morning for work. Look, this is nothing.
We need this van. Leave the keys, step out and walk away.
Next morning.

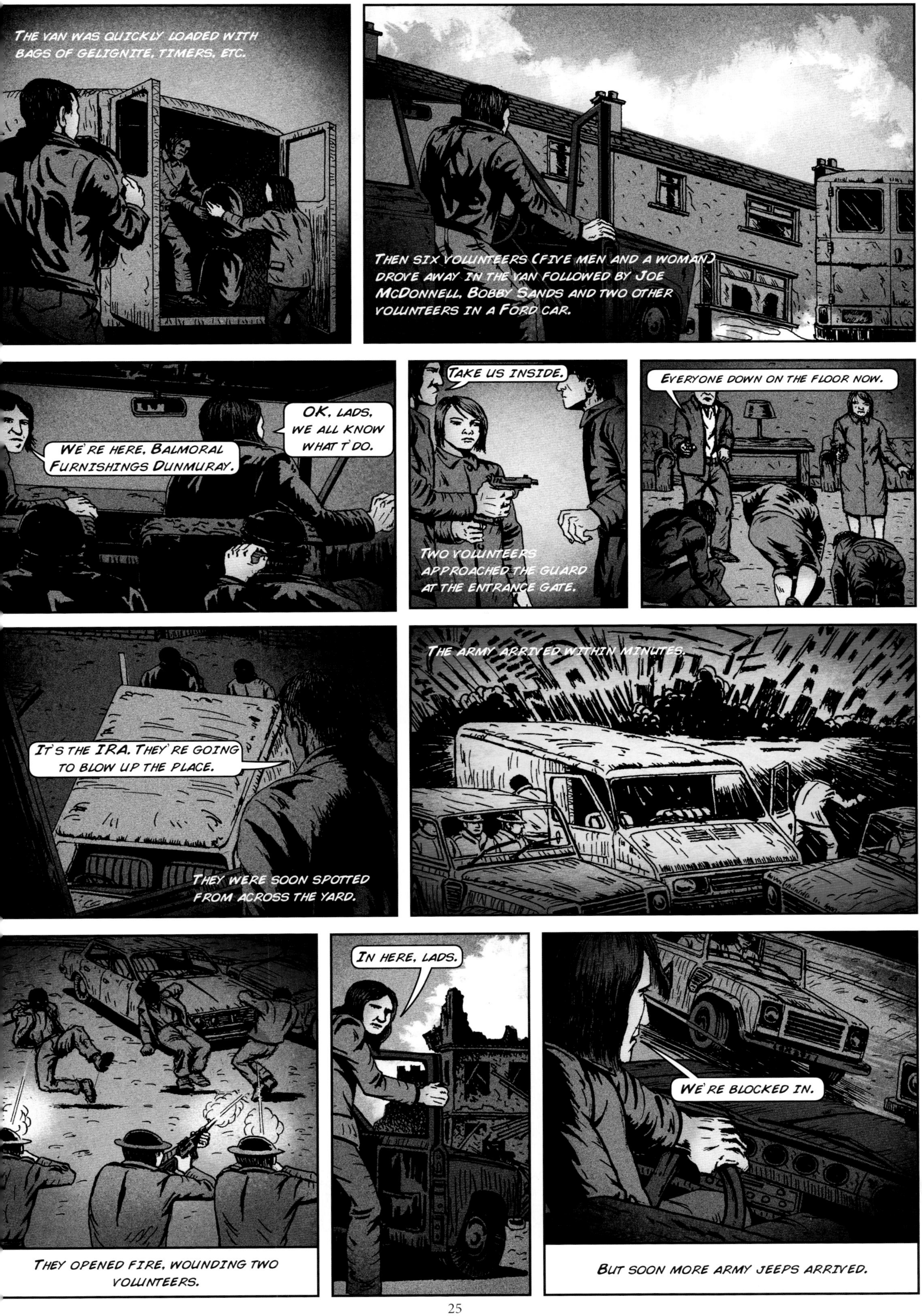
THE VAN WAS QUICKLY LOADED WITH BAGS OF GELIGNITE, TIMERS, ETC.
THEN SIX VOLUNTEERS (FIVE MEN AND A WOMAN) DROVE AWAY IN THE VAN FOLLOWED BY JOE McDONNELL, BOBBY SANDS AND TWO OTHER VOLUNTEERS IN A FORD CAR.
OK, LADS, WE ALL KNOW WHAT T' DO.
WE'RE HERE, BALMORAL FURNISHINGS DUNMURAY.
TAKE US INSIDE.
TWO VOLUNTEERS APPROACHED THE GUARD AT THE ENTRANCE GATE.
EVERYONE DOWN ON THE FLOOR NOW.
IT'S THE IRA. THEY'RE GOING TO BLOW UP THE PLACE.
THEY WERE SOON SPOTTED FROM ACROSS THE YARD.
THE ARMY ARRIVED WITHIN MINUTES.
THEY OPENED FIRE, WOUNDING TWO VOLUNTEERS.
IN HERE, LADS.
WE'RE BLOCKED IN.
BUT SOON MORE ARMY JEEPS ARRIVED.

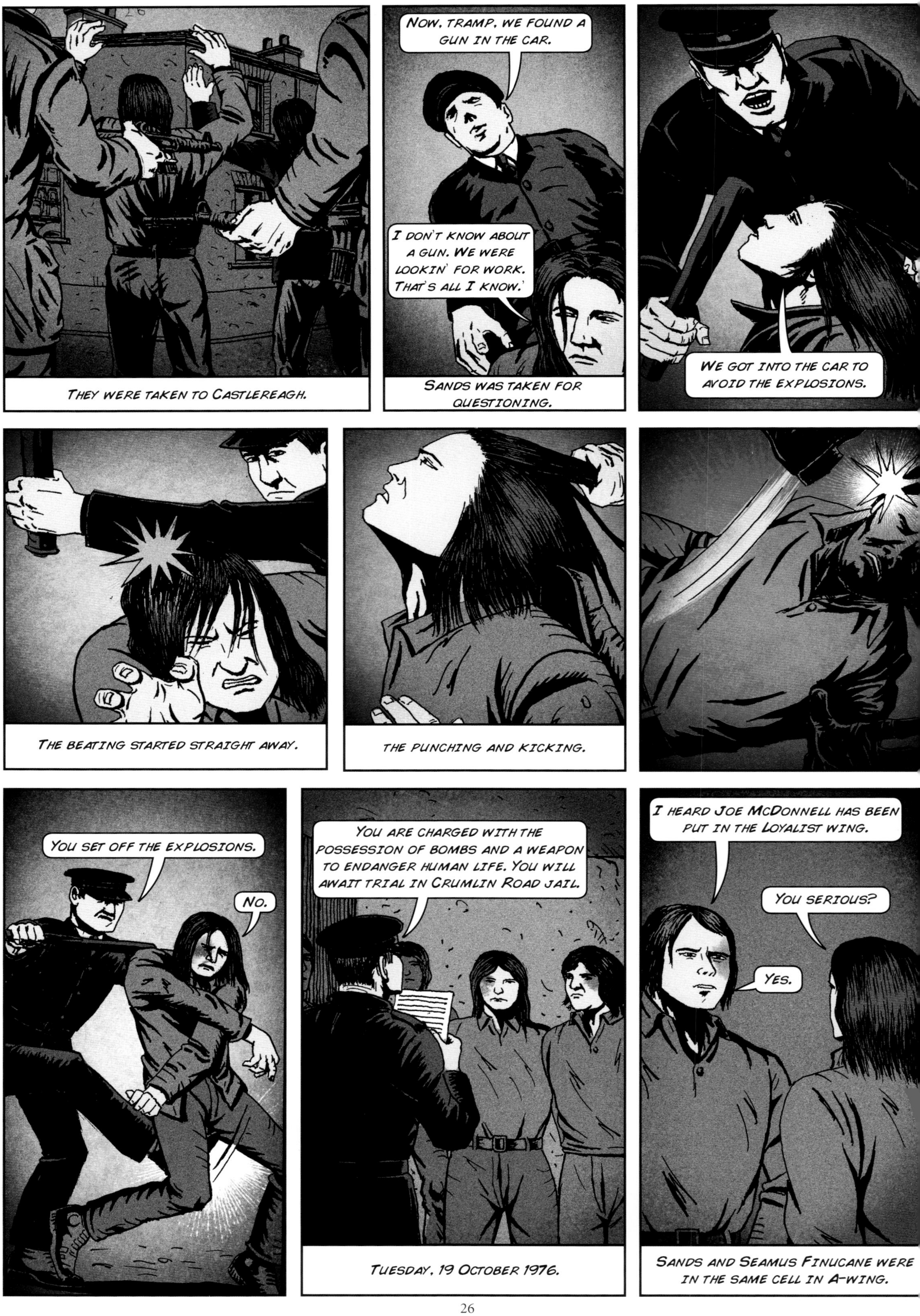
They were taken to Castlereagh.
Now, tramp, we found a gun in the car.
I don't know about a gun. We were lookin' for work. That's all I know.
Sands was taken for questioning.
We got into the car to avoid the explosions.
The beating started straight away.
the punching and kicking.
You set off the explosions.
No.
You are charged with the possession of bombs and a weapon to endanger human life. You will await trial in Crumlin Road jail.
Tuesday, 19 October 1976.
I heard Joe McDonnell has been put in the Loyalist wing.
You serious?
Yes.
Sands and Seamus Finucane were in the same cell in A-wing.

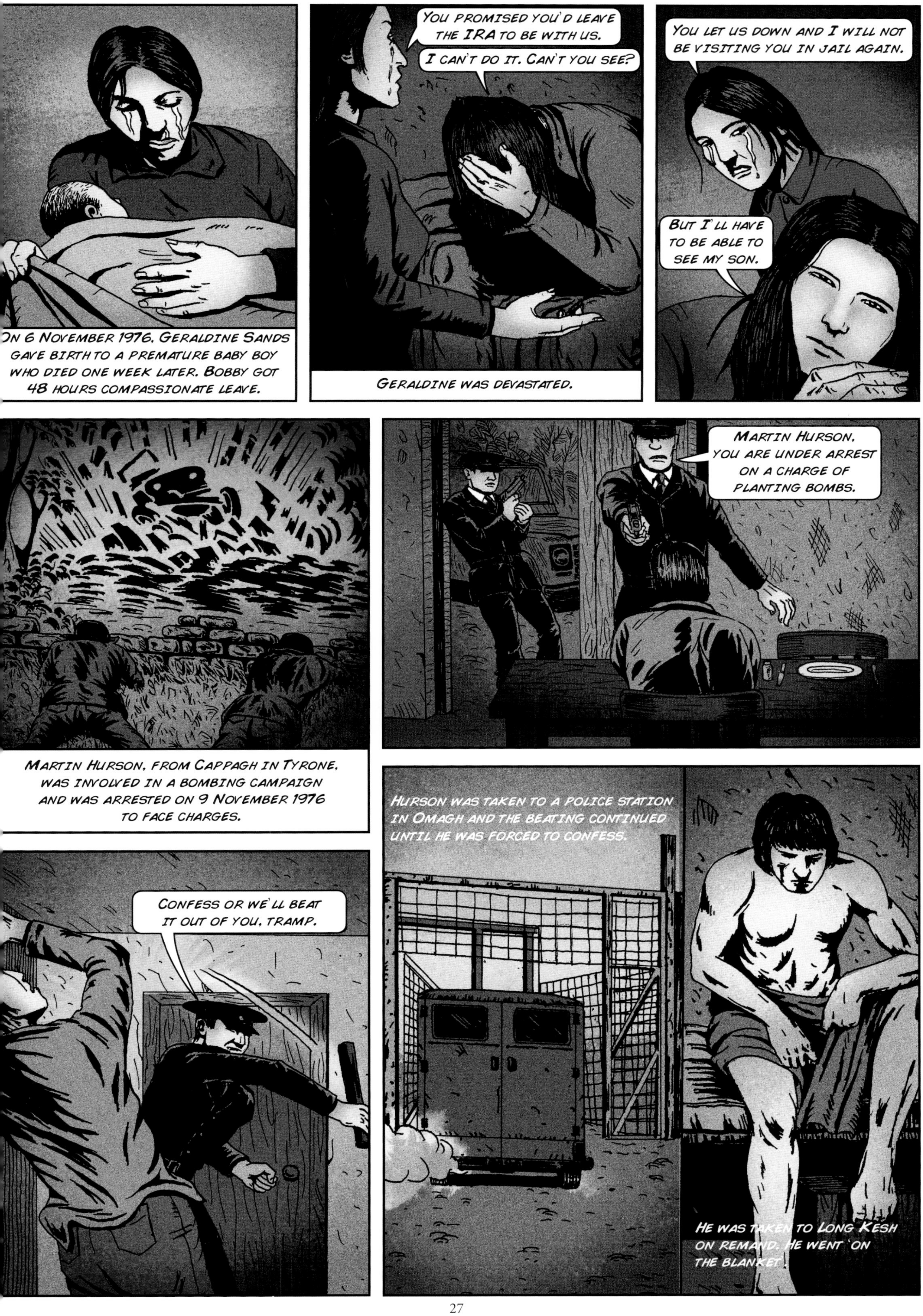
On 6 November 1976, Geraldine Sands gave birth to a premature baby boy who died one week later. Bobby got 48 hours compassionate leave.
You promised you'd leave the IRA to be with us.
I can't do it. Can't you see?
Geraldine was devastated.
You let us down and I will not be visiting you in jail again.
But I'll have to be able to see my son.
Martin Hurson, from Cappagh in Tyrone, was involved in a bombing campaign and was arrested on 9 November 1976 to face charges.
Martin Hurson, you are under arrest on a charge of planting bombs.
Confess or we'll beat it out of you, tramp.
Hurson was taken to a police station in Omagh and the beating continued until he was forced to confess.
He was taken to Long Kesh on remand. He went 'on the blanket'.

WE REFUSE TO RECOGNISE THIS COURT.

I FIND YOU GUILTY AS CHARGED AND I SENTENCE EACH OF YOU TO 14 YEARS IN PRISON.

THE TRIAL OF JOE MCDONNELL, BOBBY SANDS, SEAMUS FINUCANE AND SEAN LAVERY WAS HELD ON 5 SEPTEMBER 1977.

WHEN SENTENCE WAS PASSED BOBBY SANDS STOOD TO WAVE TO HIS MOTHER, ROSALEEN, AND HIS SISTER, MARCELLA.

MOVE IN, TRAMP!

WITH ONLY FOUR WARDERS PRESENT, A SAVAGE FIGHT BROKE OUT IN THE COURTROOM.

PUT THESE ON.

WE'RE NOT WEARING PRISON CLOTHES.

WE'RE POLITICAL PRISONERS.

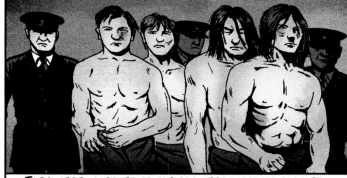

THEY WERE MARCHED TO THE SHOWERS WITH NO CLOTHES, JUST A TOWEL TO COVER THEM.

THEN THREE DAYS OF CELLULAR CONFINEMENT.

A STARVATION DIET OF TWO SCOOPS OF POTATO AND A LADLE OF SOUP ON A STEEL PLATE SO HOT THEY COULD NOT TOUCH IT.

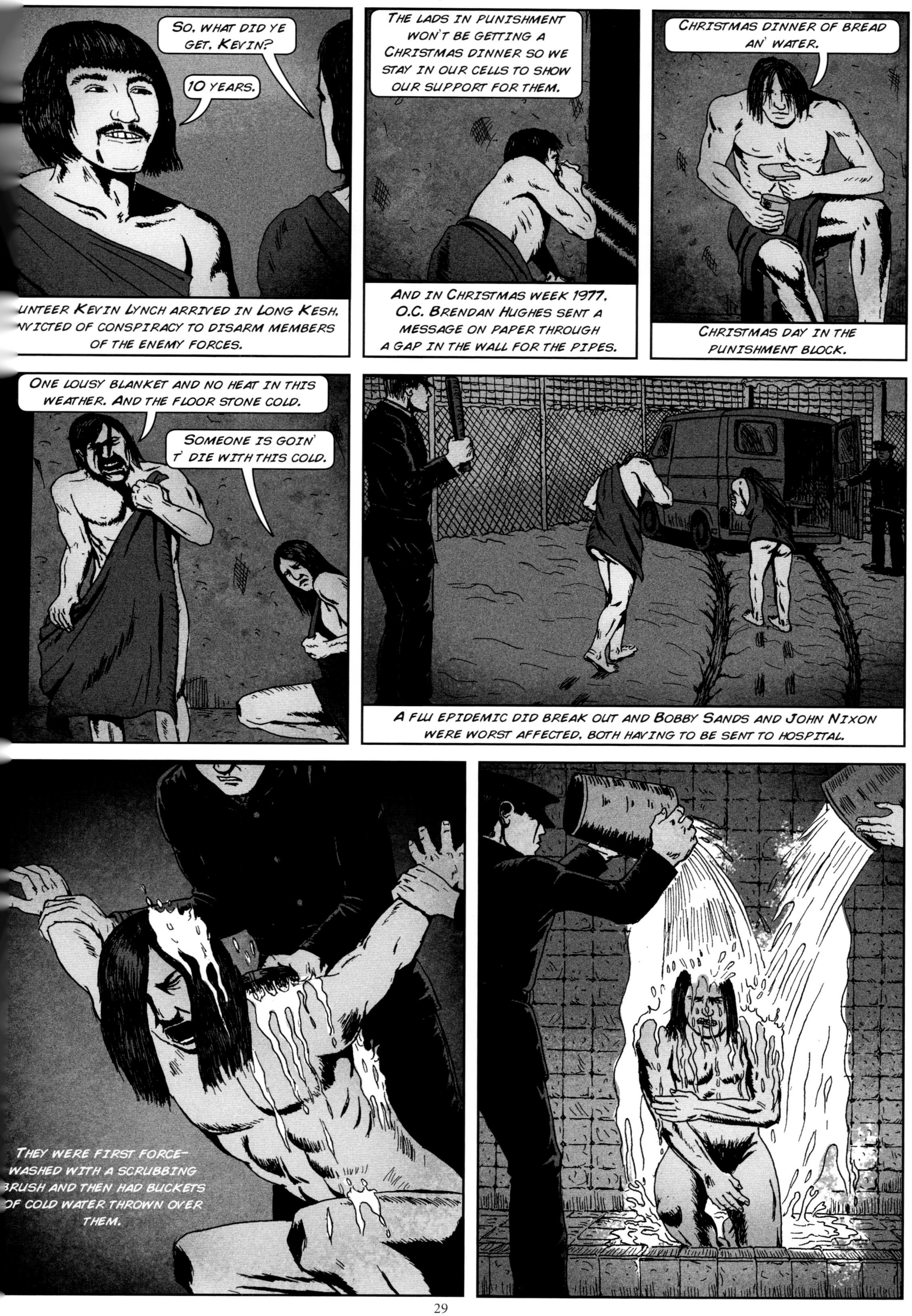
SO, WHAT DID YE GET, KEVIN?
10 YEARS.
UNTEER KEVIN LYNCH ARRIVED IN LONG KESH, NVICTED OF CONSPIRACY TO DISARM MEMBERS OF THE ENEMY FORCES.
THE LADS IN PUNISHMENT WON'T BE GETTING A CHRISTMAS DINNER SO WE STAY IN OUR CELLS TO SHOW OUR SUPPORT FOR THEM.
AND IN CHRISTMAS WEEK 1977, O.C. BRENDAN HUGHES SENT A MESSAGE ON PAPER THROUGH A GAP IN THE WALL FOR THE PIPES.
CHRISTMAS DINNER OF BREAD AN' WATER.
CHRISTMAS DAY IN THE PUNISHMENT BLOCK.
ONE LOUSY BLANKET AND NO HEAT IN THIS WEATHER. AND THE FLOOR STONE COLD.
SOMEONE IS GOIN' T' DIE WITH THIS COLD.
A FLU EPIDEMIC DID BREAK OUT AND BOBBY SANDS AND JOHN NIXON WERE WORST AFFECTED, BOTH HAVING TO BE SENT TO HOSPITAL.
THEY WERE FIRST FORCE-WASHED WITH A SCRUBBING RUSH AND THEN HAD BUCKETS OF COLD WATER THROWN OVER THEM.

AFTER HOSPITAL, SANDS WAS IN A WING AND HEARING THE CALL 'BEARS IN THE AIR' HE PEEPED THROUGH A SMALL HOLE AND SAW 18 YEAR OLD PEE-WEE O'DONNELL BEING PULLED FROM HIS CELL.

BEND OVER.

IT'S THE PUNISHMENT BLOCK FOR YOU FOR ASSAULTING A PRISON OFFICER.

BADLY BEATEN, PEE-WEE WAS LED AWAY.

WE'RE SHORT A FEW FISH. THERE'S NONE FOR YOU. I'LL TELL THE COOK.

AT MEALTIME, BOBBY SANDS' DOOR OPENED.

ONE COLD HARD POTATO AND ABOUT 40 PEAS.

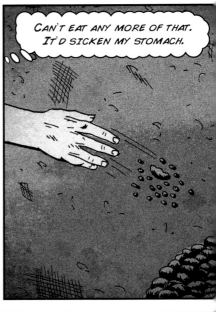

CAN'T EAT ANY MORE OF THAT. IT'D SICKEN MY STOMACH.

BOBBY TOOK TO WRITING TO HELP HIM OVER HIS DEPRESSION AT NOT SEEING GERALDINE FOLLOWING THEIR BREAK-UP.

RANG ANOIS!

IRISH CLASS. GOOD.

AN...A N BHUIL B H FU I L'

WHEN THE SHOUT CAME EVERYONE GOT READY FOR THE NIGHTLY IRISH CLASS. EACH WORD WAS SPELT OUT AND WRITTEN DOWN.

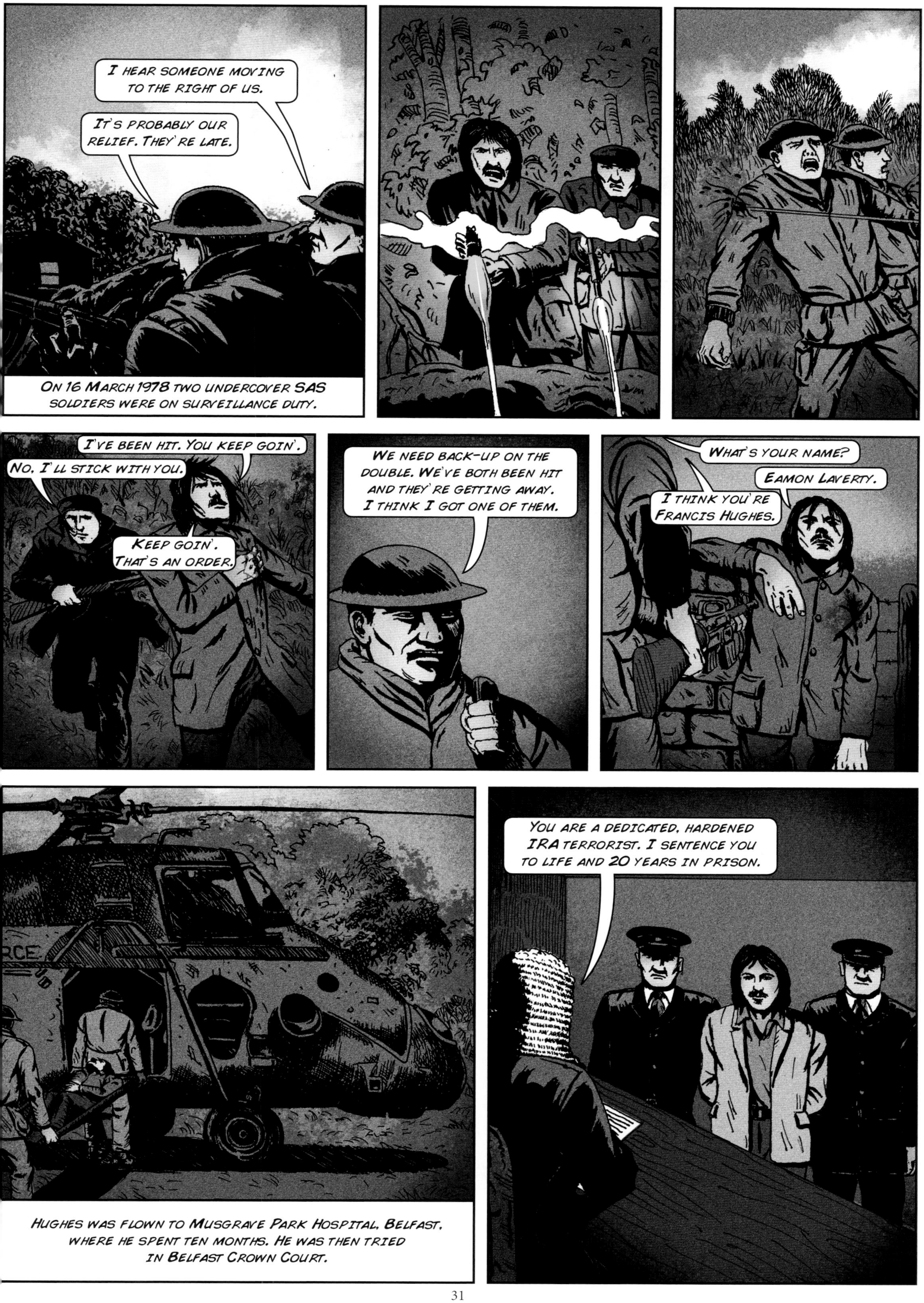
I HEAR SOMEONE MOVING TO THE RIGHT OF US.
IT'S PROBABLY OUR RELIEF. THEY'RE LATE.
ON 16 MARCH 1978 TWO UNDERCOVER SAS SOLDIERS WERE ON SURVEILLANCE DUTY.
I'VE BEEN HIT. YOU KEEP GOIN'.
NO. I'LL STICK WITH YOU.
KEEP GOIN'. THAT'S AN ORDER.
WE NEED BACK-UP ON THE DOUBLE. WE'VE BOTH BEEN HIT AND THEY'RE GETTING AWAY. I THINK I GOT ONE OF THEM.
WHAT'S YOUR NAME?
EAMON LAVERTY.
I THINK YOU'RE FRANCIS HUGHES.
HUGHES WAS FLOWN TO MUSGRAVE PARK HOSPITAL, BELFAST, WHERE HE SPENT TEN MONTHS. HE WAS THEN TRIED IN BELFAST CROWN COURT.
YOU ARE A DEDICATED, HARDENED IRA TERRORIST. I SENTENCE YOU TO LIFE AND 20 YEARS IN PRISON.

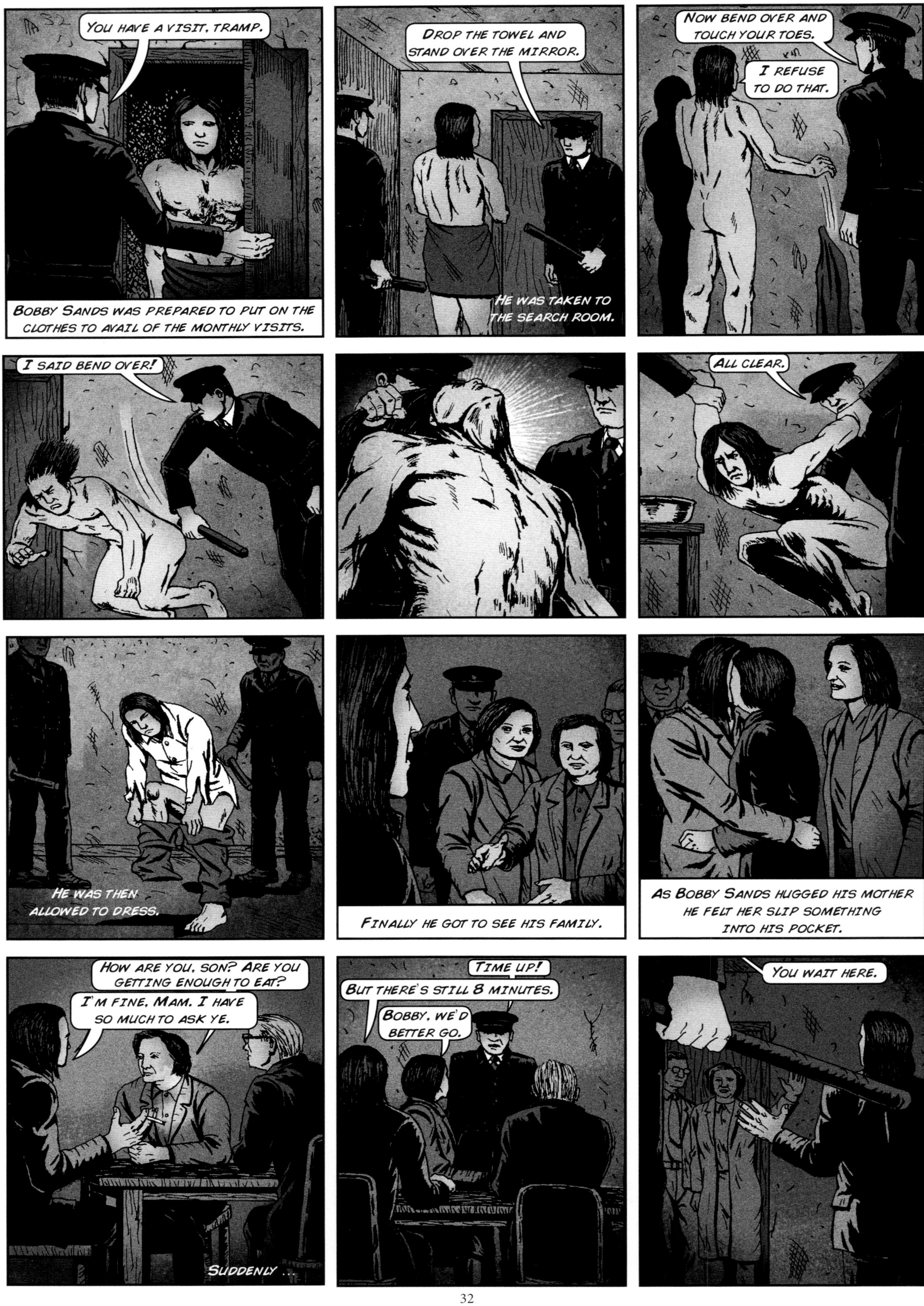
You have a visit, tramp.
Bobby Sands was prepared to put on the clothes to avail of the monthly visits.
Drop the towel and stand over the mirror.
He was taken to the search room.
Now bend over and touch your toes.
I refuse to do that.
I said bend over!
All clear.
He was then allowed to dress.
Finally he got to see his family.
As Bobby Sands hugged his mother he felt her slip something into his pocket.
How are you, son? Are you getting enough to eat?
I'm fine, Mam. I have so much to ask ye.
Suddenly ...
Time up!
But there's still 8 minutes.
Bobby, we'd better go.
You wait here.

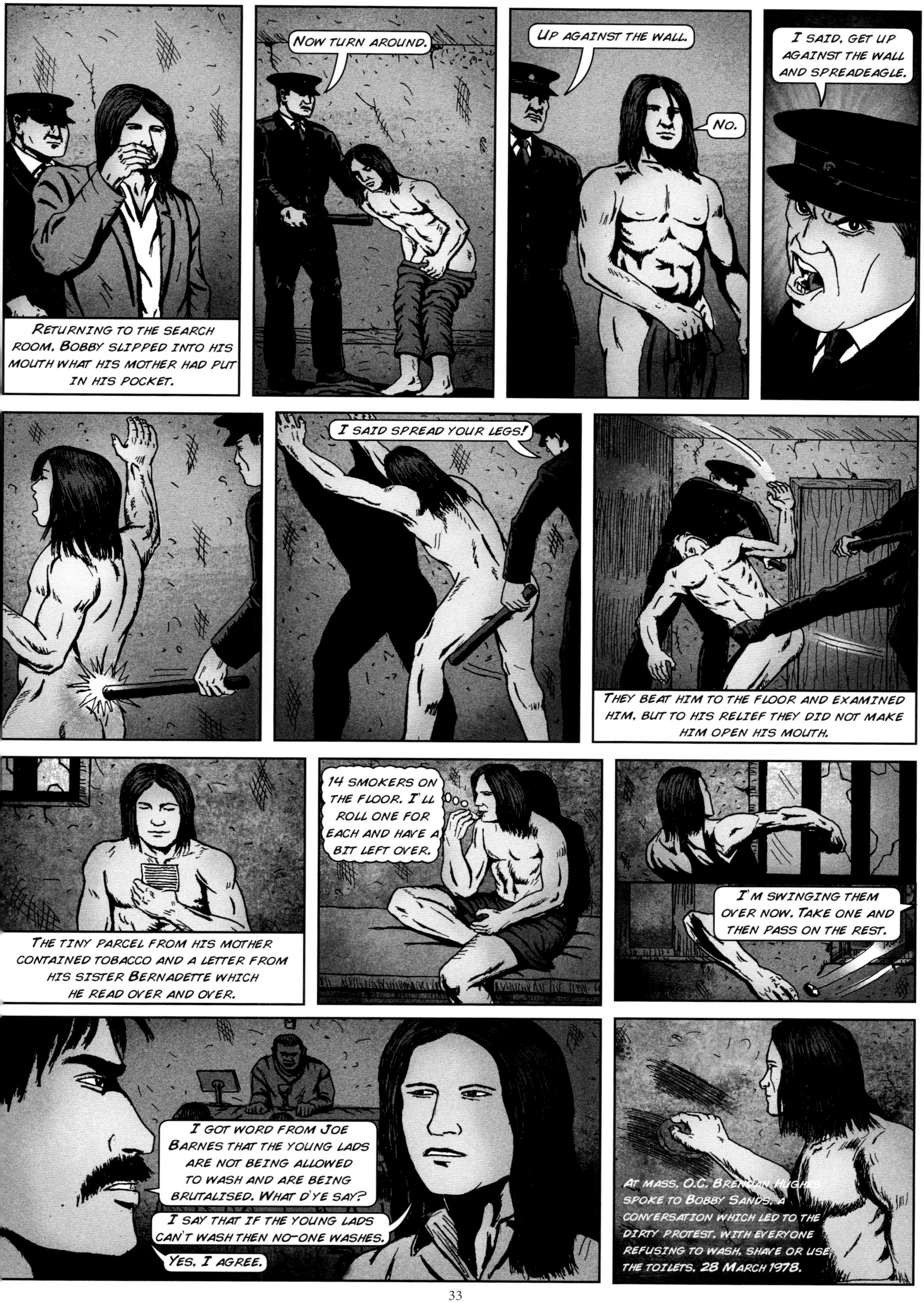

Returning to the search room, Bobby slipped into his mouth what his mother had put in his pocket.
Now turn around.
Up against the wall.
No.
I said, get up against the wall and spreadeagle.
I said spread your legs!
They beat him to the floor and examined him, but to his relief they did not make him open his mouth.
The tiny parcel from his mother contained tobacco and a letter from his sister Bernadette which he read over and over.
14 smokers on the floor. I'll roll one for each and have a bit left over.
I'm swinging them over now. Take one and then pass on the rest.
I got word from Joe Barnes that the young lads are not being allowed to wash and are being brutalised. What d'ye say?
I say that if the young lads can't wash then no-one washes.
Yes, I agree.
At mass, O.C. Brendan Hughes spoke to Bobby Sands, a conversation which led to the dirty protest, with everyone refusing to wash, shave or use the toilets, 28 March 1978.

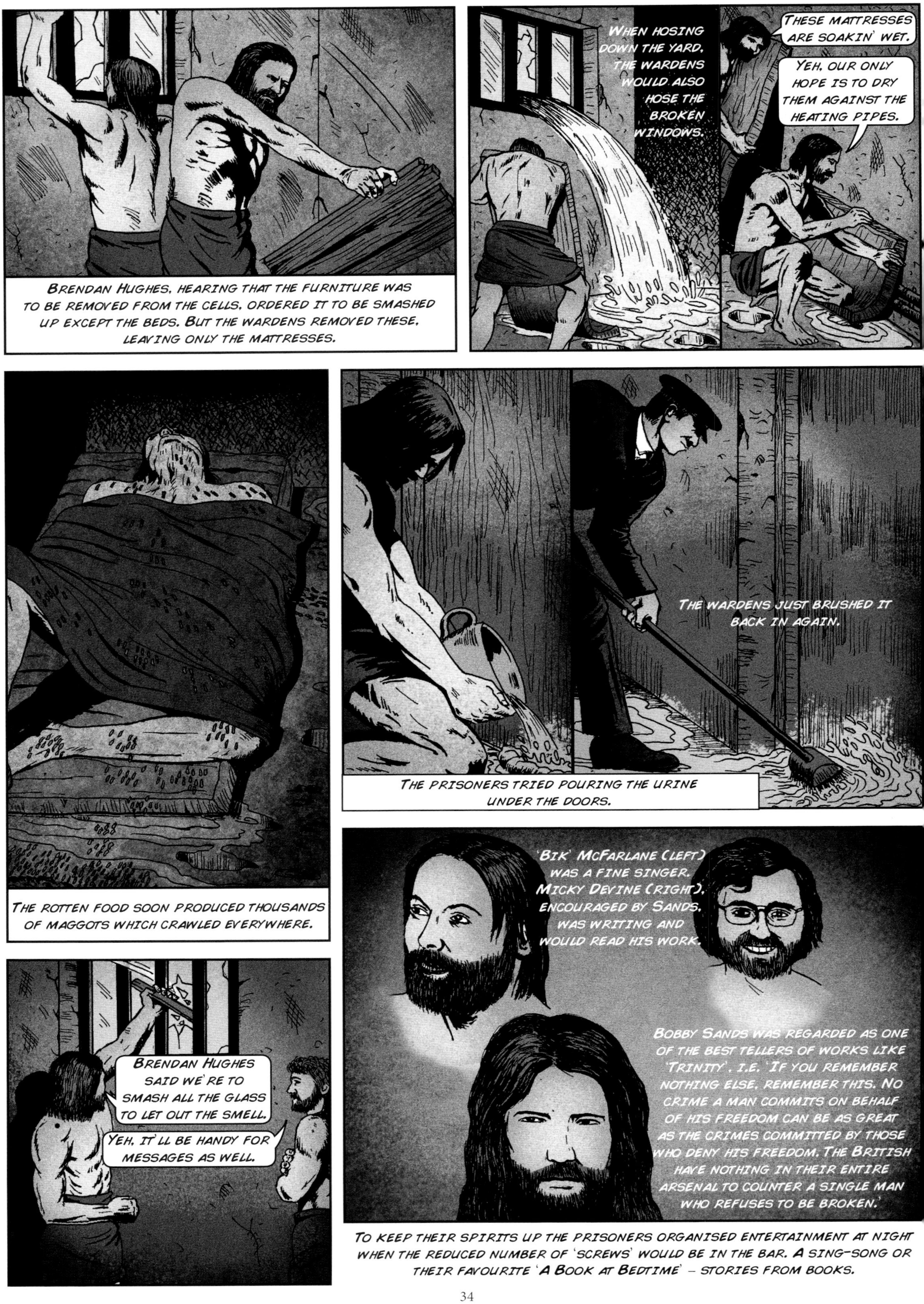
BRENDAN HUGHES, HEARING THAT THE FURNITURE WAS TO BE REMOVED FROM THE CELLS, ORDERED IT TO BE SMASHED UP EXCEPT THE BEDS. BUT THE WARDENS REMOVED THESE, LEAVING ONLY THE MATTRESSES.
WHEN HOSING DOWN THE YARD, THE WARDENS WOULD ALSO HOSE THE BROKEN WINDOWS.
THESE MATTRESSES ARE SOAKIN' WET.
YEH, OUR ONLY HOPE IS TO DRY THEM AGAINST THE HEATING PIPES.
THE ROTTEN FOOD SOON PRODUCED THOUSANDS OF MAGGOTS WHICH CRAWLED EVERYWHERE.
THE PRISONERS TRIED POURING THE URINE UNDER THE DOORS.
THE WARDENS JUST BRUSHED IT BACK IN AGAIN.
BRENDAN HUGHES SAID WE'RE TO SMASH ALL THE GLASS TO LET OUT THE SMELL.
YEH, IT'LL BE HANDY FOR MESSAGES AS WELL.
'BIK' McFARLANE (LEFT) WAS A FINE SINGER. MICKY DEVINE (RIGHT), ENCOURAGED BY SANDS, WAS WRITING AND WOULD READ HIS WORK.
BOBBY SANDS WAS REGARDED AS ONE OF THE BEST TELLERS OF WORKS LIKE 'TRINITY'. I.E. 'IF YOU REMEMBER NOTHING ELSE, REMEMBER THIS. NO CRIME A MAN COMMITS ON BEHALF OF HIS FREEDOM CAN BE AS GREAT AS THE CRIMES COMMITTED BY THOSE WHO DENY HIS FREEDOM. THE BRITISH HAVE NOTHING IN THEIR ENTIRE ARSENAL TO COUNTER A SINGLE MAN WHO REFUSES TO BE BROKEN.'
TO KEEP THEIR SPIRITS UP THE PRISONERS ORGANISED ENTERTAINMENT AT NIGHT WHEN THE REDUCED NUMBER OF 'SCREWS' WOULD BE IN THE BAR. A SING-SONG OR THEIR FAVOURITE 'A BOOK AT BEDTIME' – STORIES FROM BOOKS.

LADS, THIS IS CARDINAL Ó FIAICH, WHO HAS COME TO SEE FOR HIMSELF THE CONDITIONS IN WHICH WE ARE FORCED TO LIVE.

LADS, I CAN UNDERSTAND YE ARE PREPARED TO LIVE IN THESE HORRENDOUS CONDITIONS. YE ARE NOT CRIMINALS, I KNOW THAT.

IN JULY, CARDINAL Ó FIAICH REQUESTED A VISIT TO THE H-BLOCKS. HE WAS BROUGHT TO MARTIN HURSON'S CELL WHERE PRISONERS FROM HIS DIOCESE WERE. THEY TALKED FOR ALMOST AN HOUR. HE GAVE THEM HUNDREDS OF CIGARETTES.

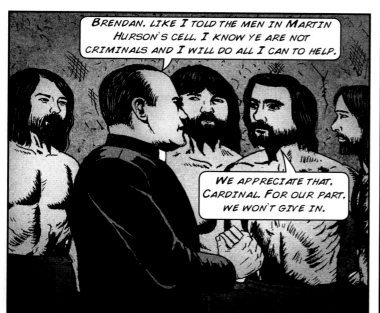

BRENDAN, LIKE I TOLD THE MEN IN MARTIN HURSON'S CELL, I KNOW YE ARE NOT CRIMINALS AND I WILL DO ALL I CAN TO HELP.

WE APPRECIATE THAT, CARDINAL. FOR OUR PART, WE WON'T GIVE IN.

IN H5, THE MEETING WAS IN BRENDAN HUGHES' CELL, WHERE HE FOUND THE SAME DETERMINATION TO KEEP IT UP UNTIL THEY WERE CLASSED AS POLITICAL PRISONERS.

THE AWFUL CONDITIONS THAT I WITNESSED YESTERDAY REMINDED ME OF THE HOMELESS PEOPLE LIVING IN THE SEWER PIPES IN CALCUTTA. THOSE LADS WOULD RATHER FACE DEATH THAN BE CLASSED AS CRIMINALS.

THE FOLLOWING DAY, HE ISSUED A STATEMENT IN WHICH HE EXPRESSED SHOCK AT THE INHUMANE CONDITIONS.

C'MON, OUT!

THEY NEED YOUR SUPPORT.

SUPPORT THE BLANKET MEN IN THE H-BLOCKS

THE PUBLIC SOON BECAME AWARE OF WHAT WAS HAPPENING IN THE H-BLOCKS AND PEOPLE LIKE BERNADETTE MCALISKEY HELD DEMONSTRATIONS AND INTERRUPTED MEETINGS SHOUTING SUPPORT FOR THE BLANKET MEN.

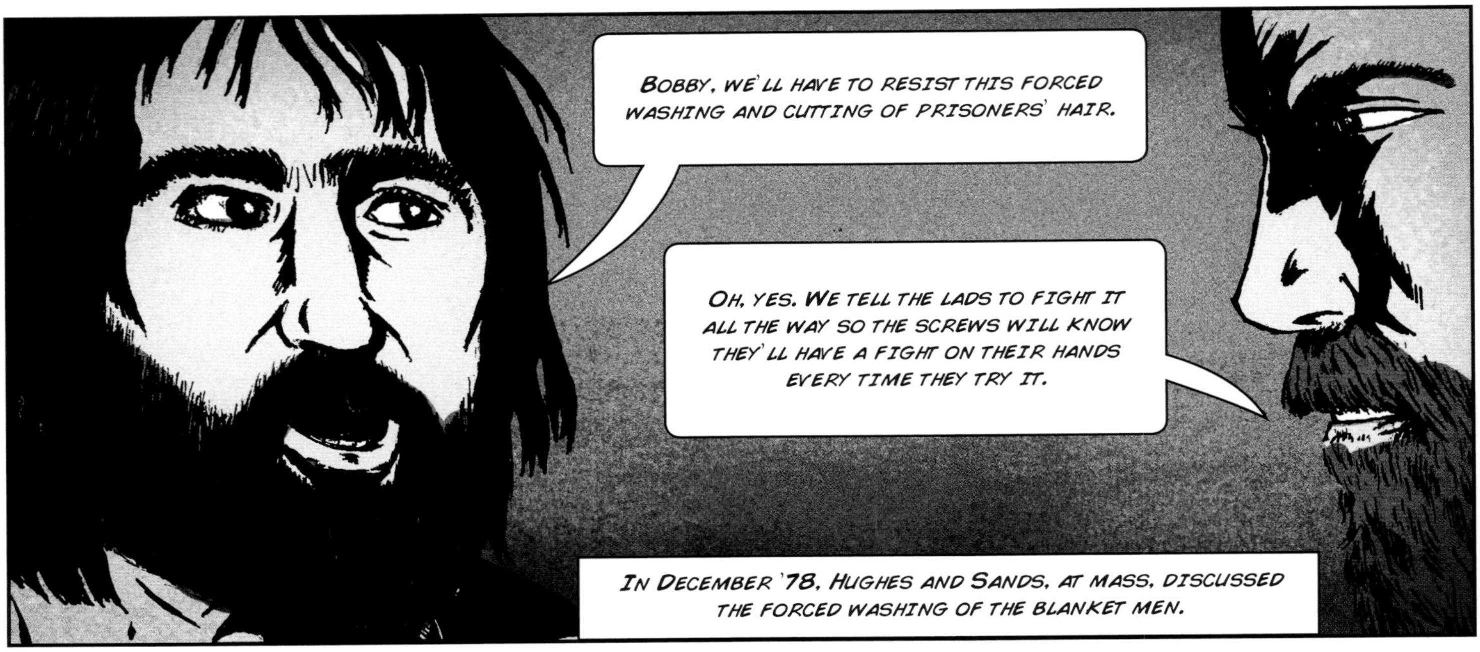
Bobby, we'll have to resist this forced washing and cutting of prisoners' hair.
Oh, yes. We tell the lads to fight it all the way so the screws will know they'll have a fight on their hands every time they try it.
In December '78, Hughes and Sands, at mass, discussed the forced washing of the blanket men.

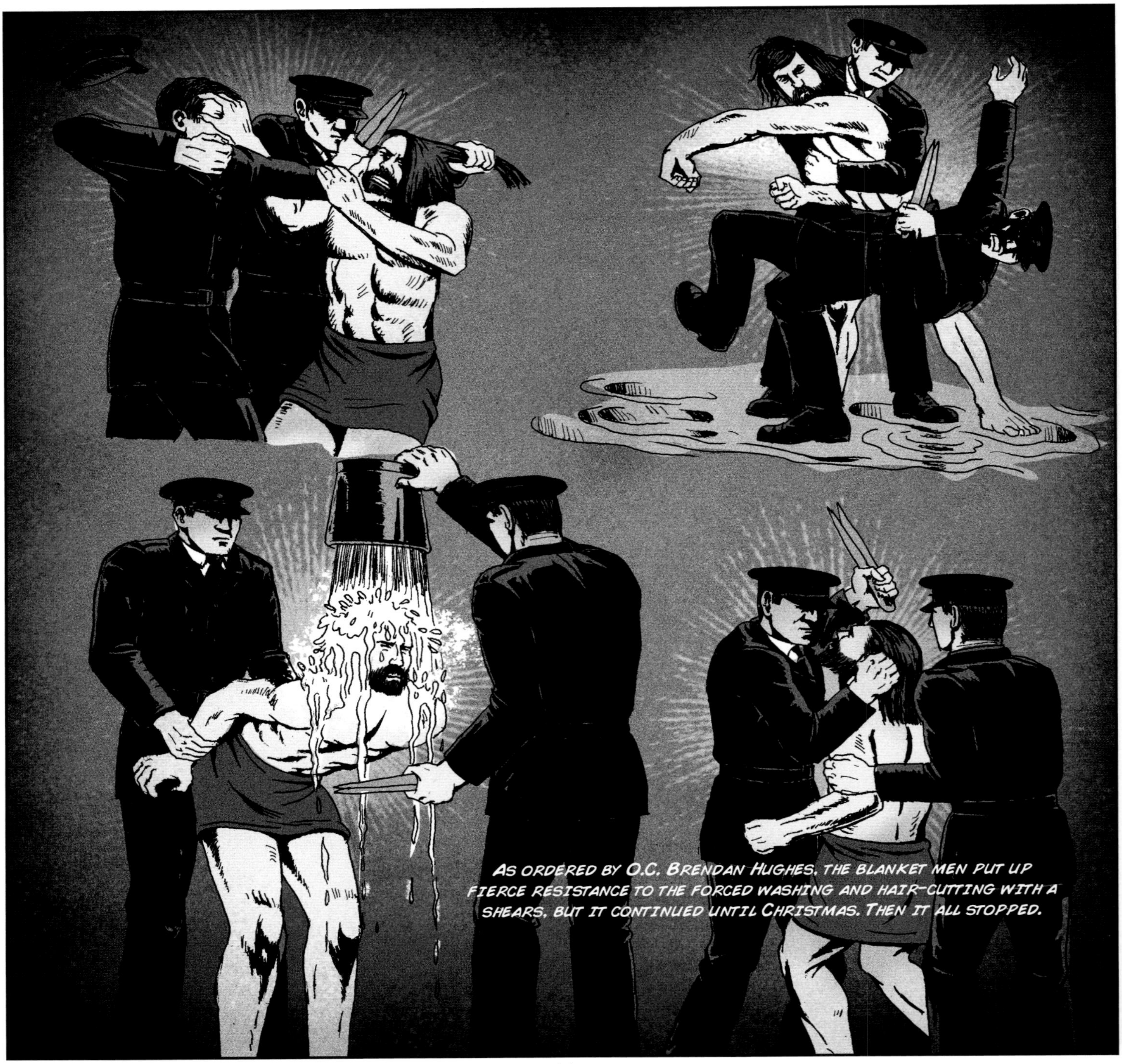
As ordered by O.C. Brendan Hughes, the blanket men put up fierce resistance to the forced washing and hair-cutting with a shears, but it continued until Christmas. Then it all stopped.

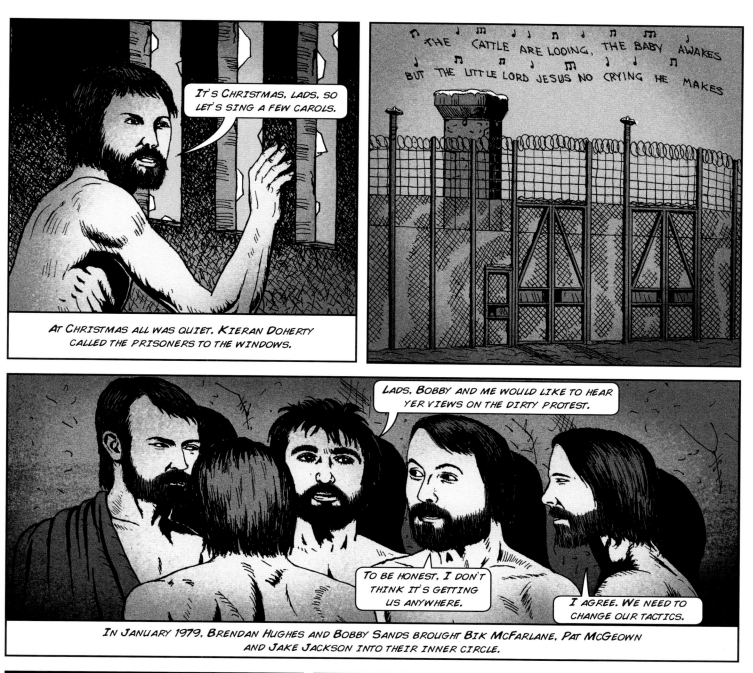

It's Christmas, lads, so let's sing a few carols.

♪ The cattle are looing, the baby awakes but the little Lord Jesus no crying he makes ♪

At Christmas all was quiet. Kieran Doherty called the prisoners to the windows.

Lads, Bobby and me would like to hear yer views on the dirty protest.

To be honest, I don't think it's getting us anywhere.

I agree. We need to change our tactics.

In January 1979, Brendan Hughes and Bobby Sands brought Bik McFarlane, Pat McGeown and Jake Jackson into their inner circle.

Bobby Sands was spending more of his time writing mainly poems and short stories.

Well, what d'ye think?

'In McIlhattan's house, the fairies are out and dancing on the hobs, the goats have collapsed, the dogs run away, there's salmon in the bogs'. It's like a song. I could put an air to it for ye.

He and Bik McFarlane became good friends. He would pass his writing on to Bik for his opinion.

37

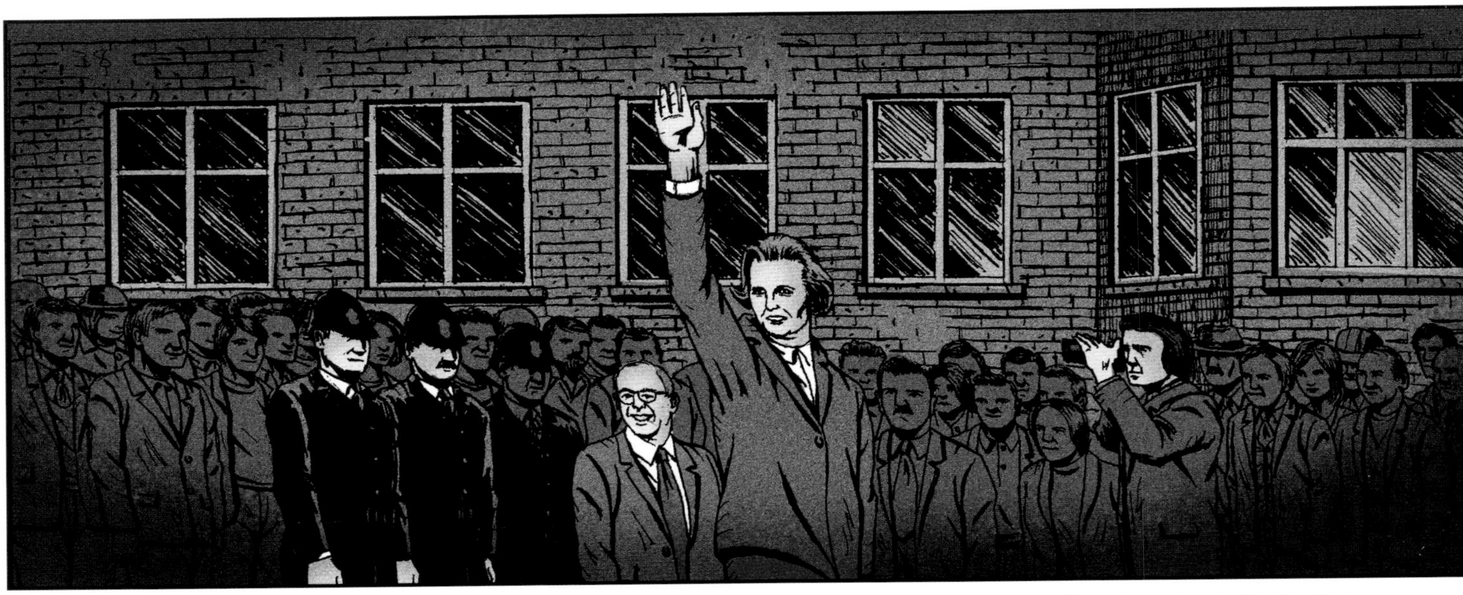

In the general elections, May 1979, Margaret Thatcher and her Conservative Party swept into power.
Bobby Sands knew the prisoners could not maintain morale much longer in the present conditions.

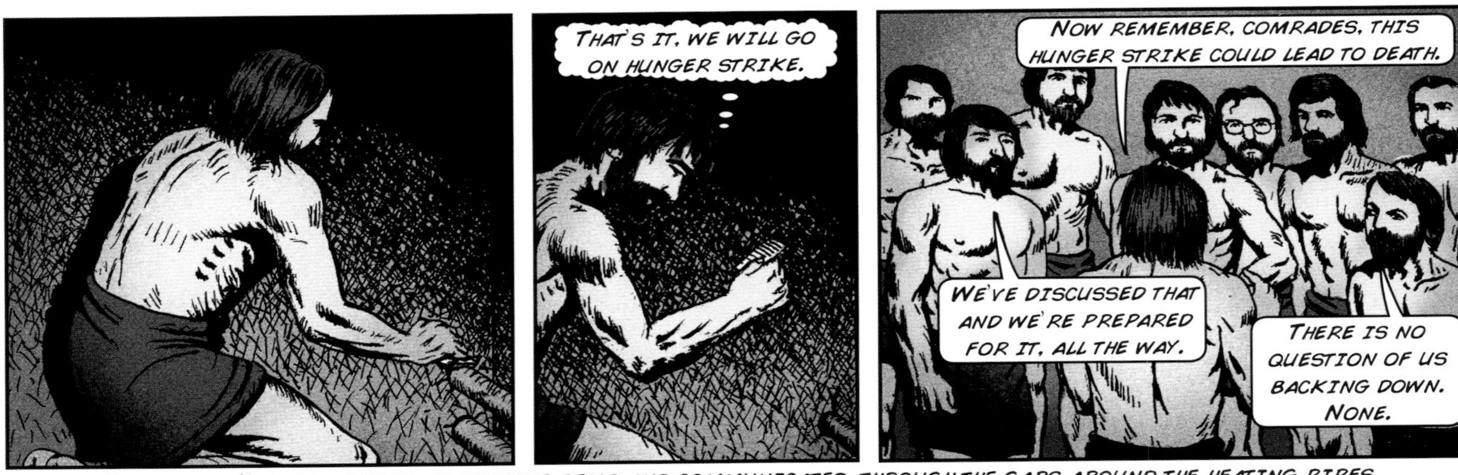

That's it, we will go on hunger strike.
Now remember, comrades, this hunger strike could lead to death.
We've discussed that and we're prepared for it, all the way.
There is no question of us backing down. None.

Sands and Hughes were in adjoining cells and communicated, through the gaps around the heating pipes, their views on what the next move should be. Soon their agreed strategy was sent to all the blanket men and they got a quick reaction from everyone contacted.

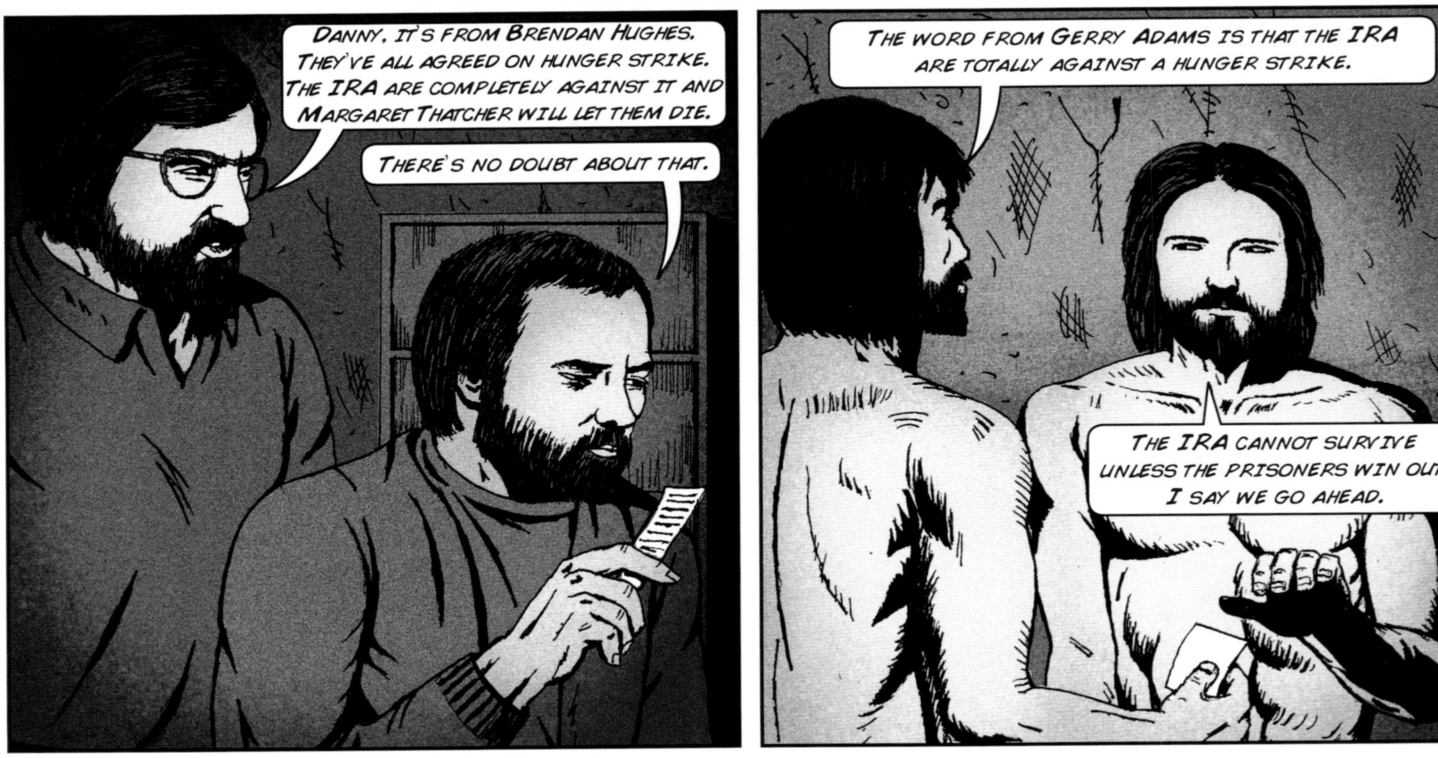

Danny, it's from Brendan Hughes. They've all agreed on hunger strike. The IRA are completely against it and Margaret Thatcher will let them die.
There's no doubt about that.
The word from Gerry Adams is that the IRA are totally against a hunger strike.
The IRA cannot survive unless the prisoners win out. I say we go ahead.

Brendan Hughes wrote to Gerry Adams telling him what had been agreed by all the prisoners.
Adams quickly let him know the reaction of the IRA, but Bobby Sands felt that the hunger strike deaths could mobilise enough support even against Thatcher. The strike would go ahead.

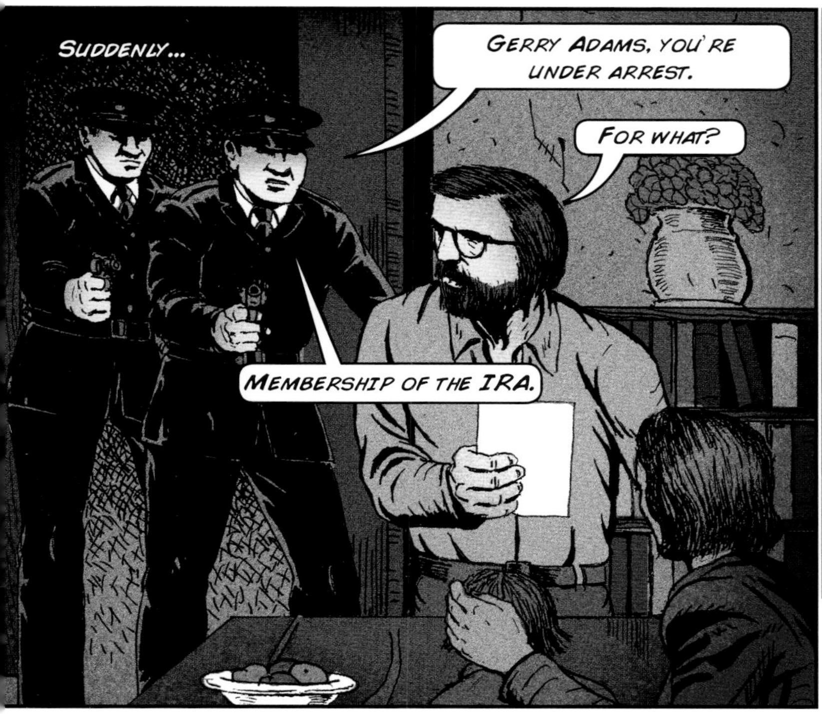
SUDDENLY...
GERRY ADAMS, YOU'RE UNDER ARREST.
FOR WHAT?
MEMBERSHIP OF THE IRA.

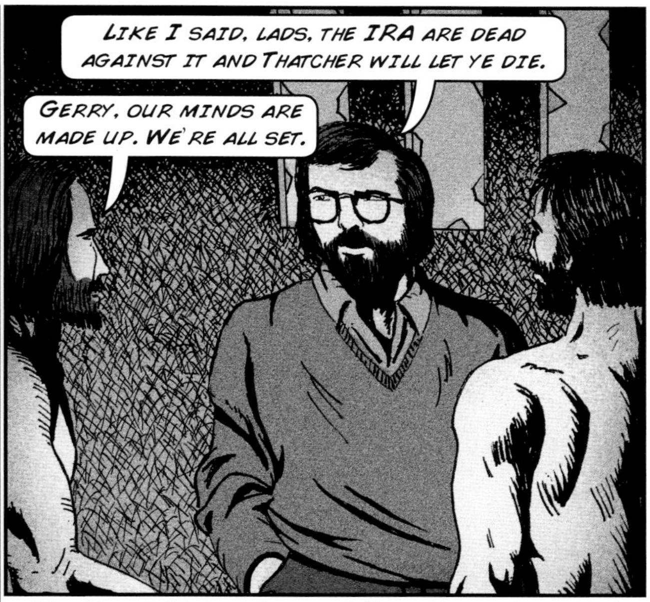
LIKE I SAID, LADS, THE IRA ARE DEAD AGAINST IT AND THATCHER WILL LET YE DIE.
GERRY, OUR MINDS ARE MADE UP. WE'RE ALL SET.

ADAMS WAS REMANDED TO THE H-BLOCKS WHERE HE MET SANDS AND HUGHES WHO WERE THINKING ABOUT HUNGER STRIKING. AFTER SIX MONTHS HE WAS ACQUITTED OF AN IRA-MEMBERSHIP CHARGE.

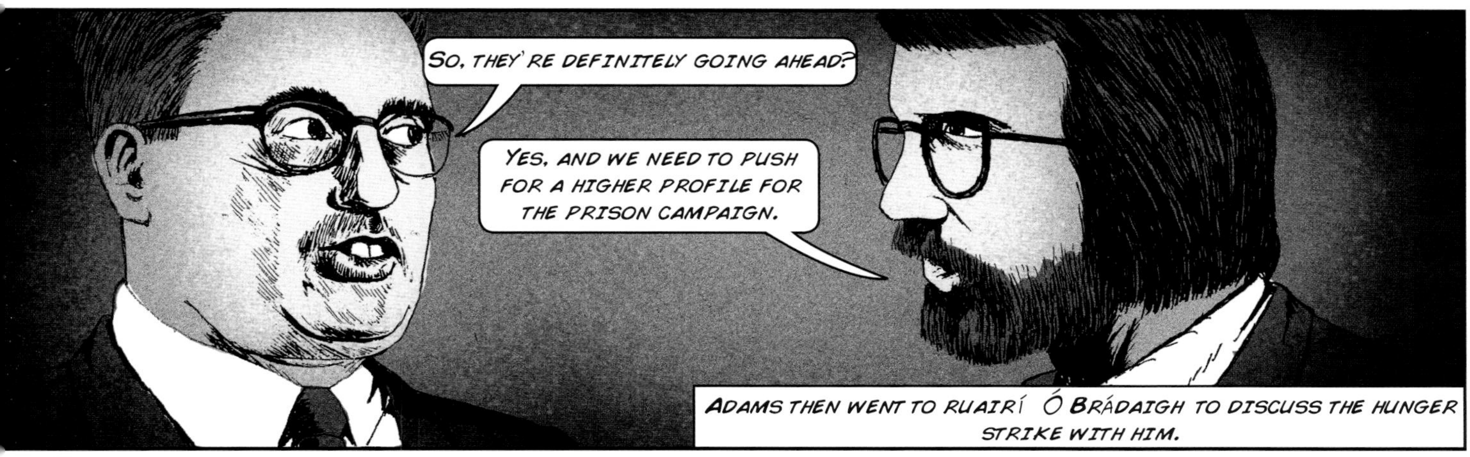
SO, THEY'RE DEFINITELY GOING AHEAD?
YES, AND WE NEED TO PUSH FOR A HIGHER PROFILE FOR THE PRISON CAMPAIGN.
ADAMS THEN WENT TO RUAIRÍ Ó BRÁDAIGH TO DISCUSS THE HUNGER STRIKE WITH HIM.

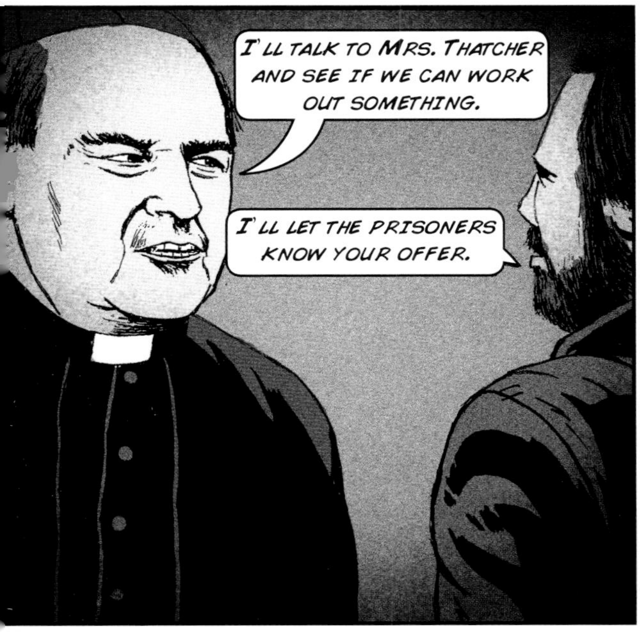
I'LL TALK TO MRS. THATCHER AND SEE IF WE CAN WORK OUT SOMETHING.
I'LL LET THE PRISONERS KNOW YOUR OFFER.

CARDINAL Ó FIAICH OFFERED TO NEGOTIATE WITH MARGARET THATCHER WHEN HE HEARD ABOUT THE PROPOSED HUNGER STRIKE. ON HEARING THIS, SANDS, HUGHES AND MCFARLANE DECIDED THEY SHOULD GIVE THE CARDINAL THE OPPORTUNITY TO MEET THATCHER AND SEE IF HE COULD GET SOMETHING OUT OF IT.

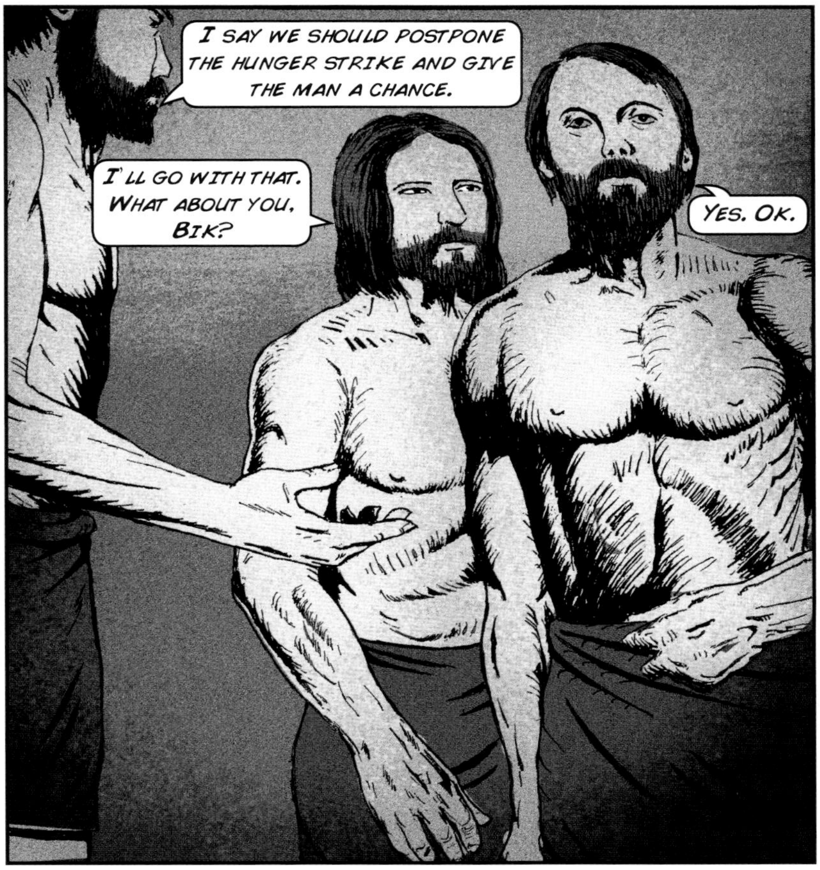
I SAY WE SHOULD POSTPONE THE HUNGER STRIKE AND GIVE THE MAN A CHANCE.
I'LL GO WITH THAT. WHAT ABOUT YOU, BIK?
YES. OK.

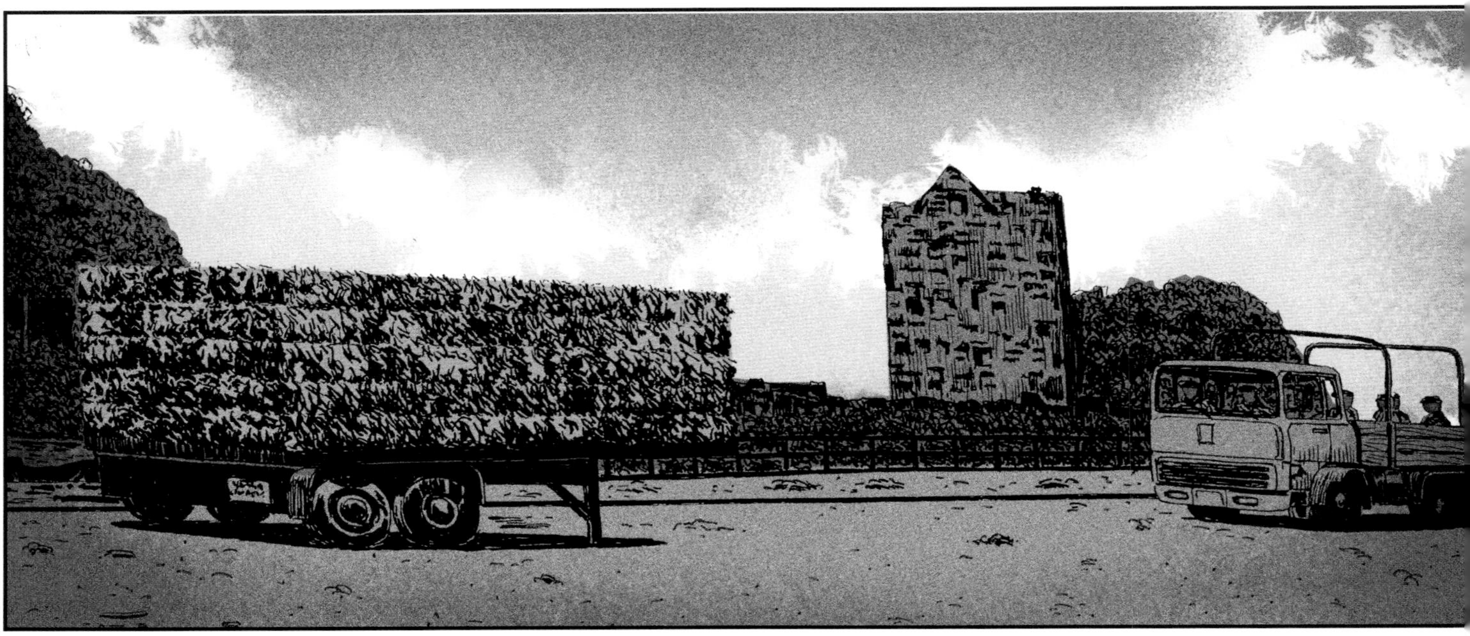

On 27 August 1979, a convoy of British soldiers was passing Narrow Water Castle, Warrenpoint.

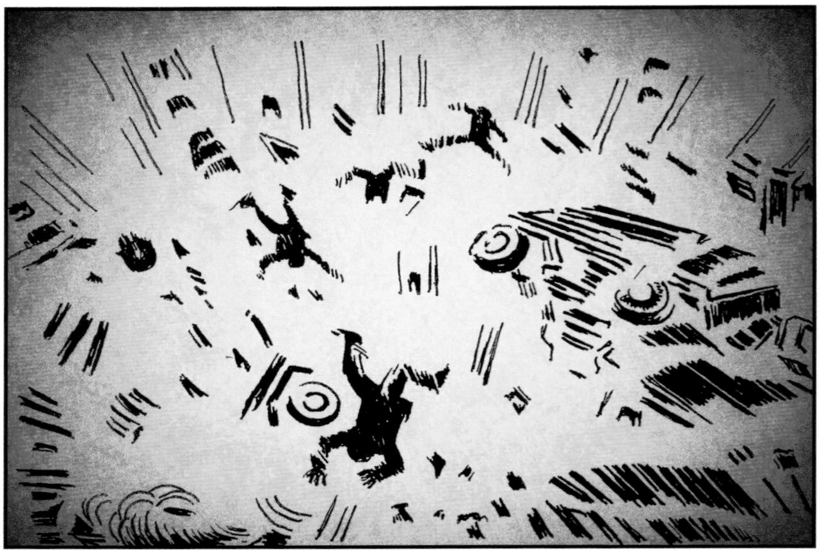

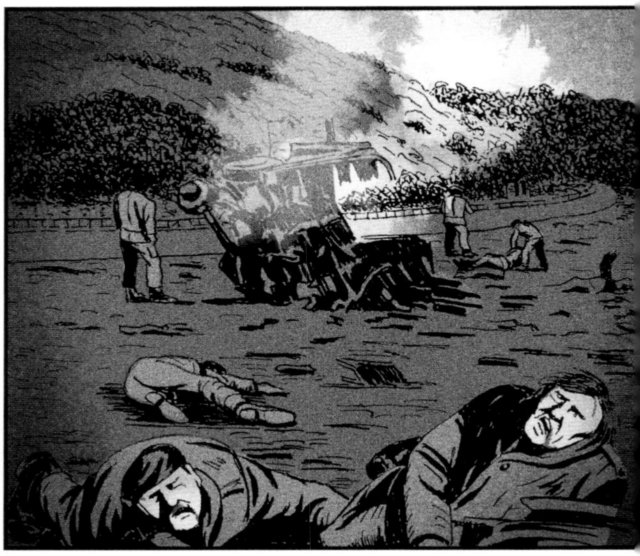

Suddenly, the IRA detonated two bombs in sequence, killing all 18 soldiers.

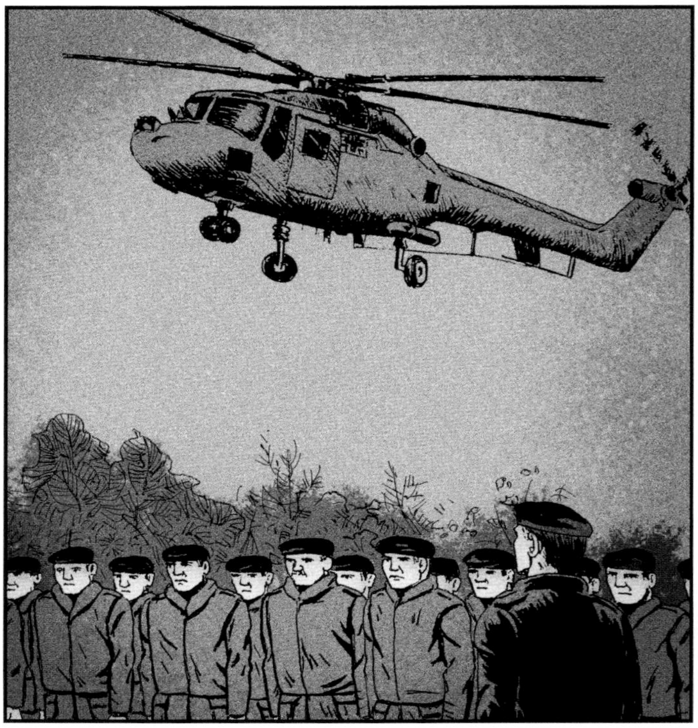

On hearing the news, Margaret Thatcher flew over to talk to the soldiers in Crossmaglen, the republican heartland.

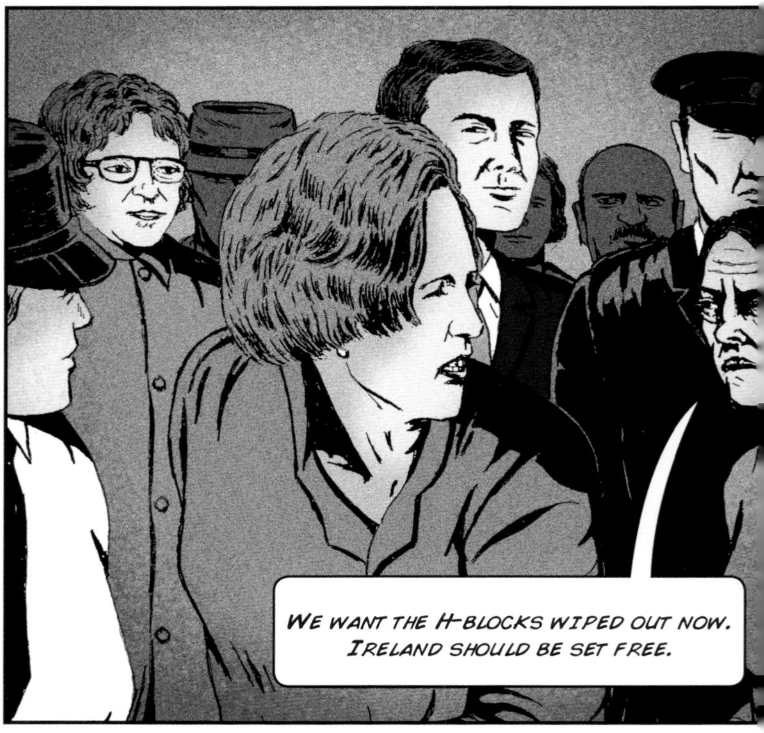
We want the H-blocks wiped out now. Ireland should be set free.

She then went walkabout in Belfast city centre, was confronted by a woman but was quickly moved on by security.

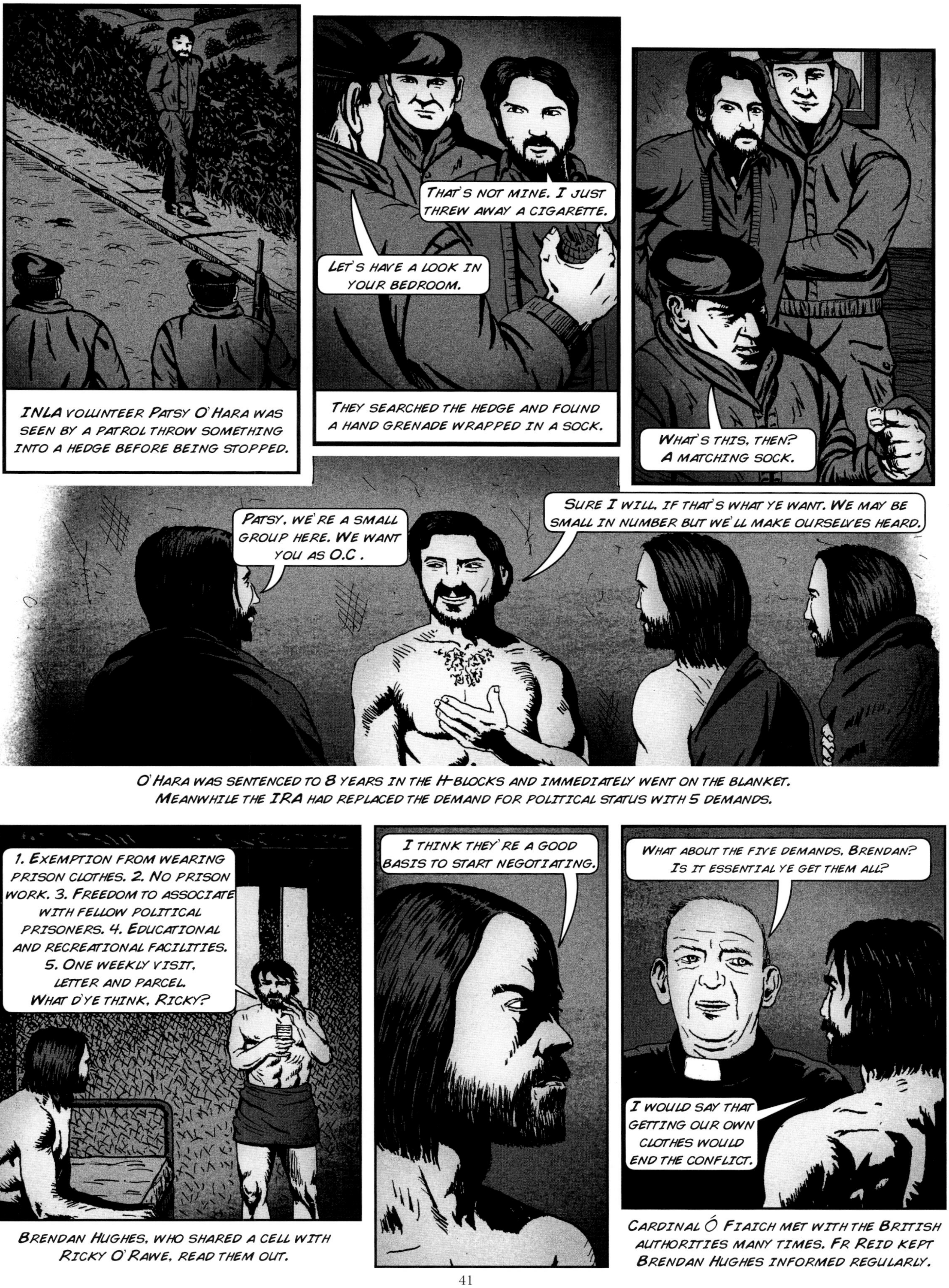
INLA VOLUNTEER PATSY O'HARA WAS SEEN BY A PATROL THROW SOMETHING INTO A HEDGE BEFORE BEING STOPPED.
THAT'S NOT MINE. I JUST THREW AWAY A CIGARETTE.
LET'S HAVE A LOOK IN YOUR BEDROOM.
THEY SEARCHED THE HEDGE AND FOUND A HAND GRENADE WRAPPED IN A SOCK.
WHAT'S THIS, THEN? A MATCHING SOCK.
PATSY, WE'RE A SMALL GROUP HERE. WE WANT YOU AS O.C .
SURE I WILL, IF THAT'S WHAT YE WANT. WE MAY BE SMALL IN NUMBER BUT WE'LL MAKE OURSELVES HEARD.
O'HARA WAS SENTENCED TO 8 YEARS IN THE H-BLOCKS AND IMMEDIATELY WENT ON THE BLANKET. MEANWHILE THE IRA HAD REPLACED THE DEMAND FOR POLITICAL STATUS WITH 5 DEMANDS.
1. EXEMPTION FROM WEARING PRISON CLOTHES. 2. NO PRISON WORK. 3. FREEDOM TO ASSOCIATE WITH FELLOW POLITICAL PRISONERS. 4. EDUCATIONAL AND RECREATIONAL FACILITIES. 5. ONE WEEKLY VISIT, LETTER AND PARCEL. WHAT D'YE THINK, RICKY?
BRENDAN HUGHES, WHO SHARED A CELL WITH RICKY O'RAWE, READ THEM OUT.
I THINK THEY'RE A GOOD BASIS TO START NEGOTIATING.
WHAT ABOUT THE FIVE DEMANDS, BRENDAN? IS IT ESSENTIAL YE GET THEM ALL?
I WOULD SAY THAT GETTING OUR OWN CLOTHES WOULD END THE CONFLICT.
CARDINAL Ó FIAICH MET WITH THE BRITISH AUTHORITIES MANY TIMES. FR REID KEPT BRENDAN HUGHES INFORMED REGULARLY.

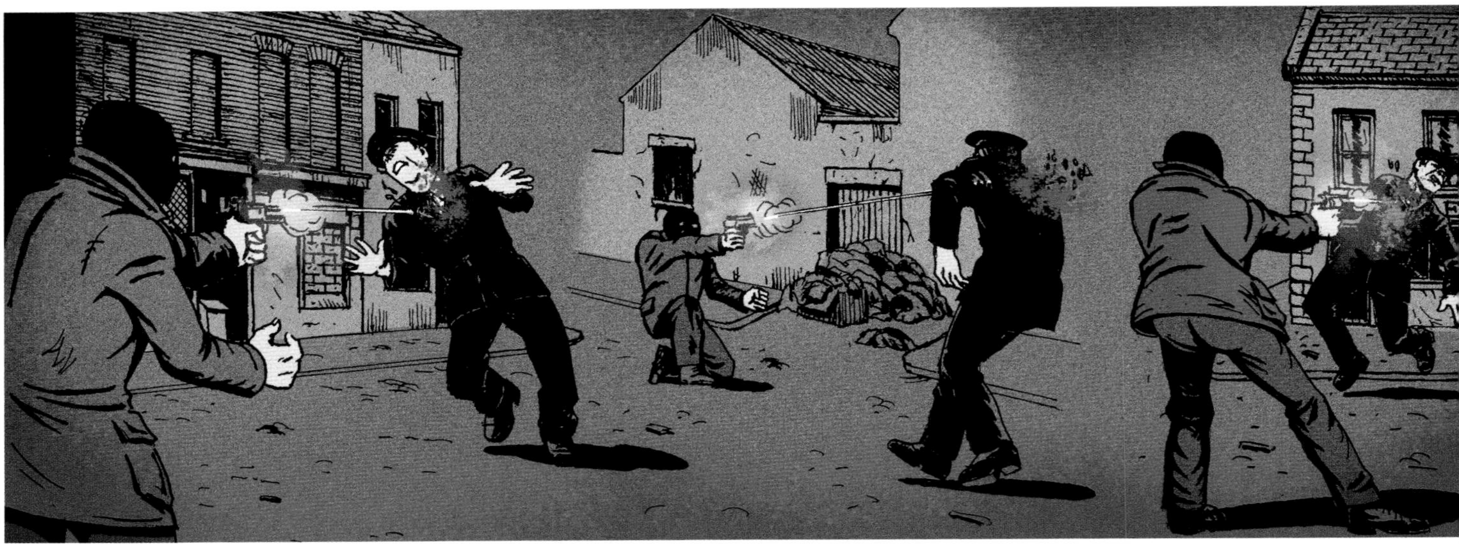

FOLLOWING THEIR THREAT THE IRA HAD, BY JANUARY 1980, KILLED 18 PRISON OFFICERS FOR ILL TREATING REPUBLICAN PRISONERS.

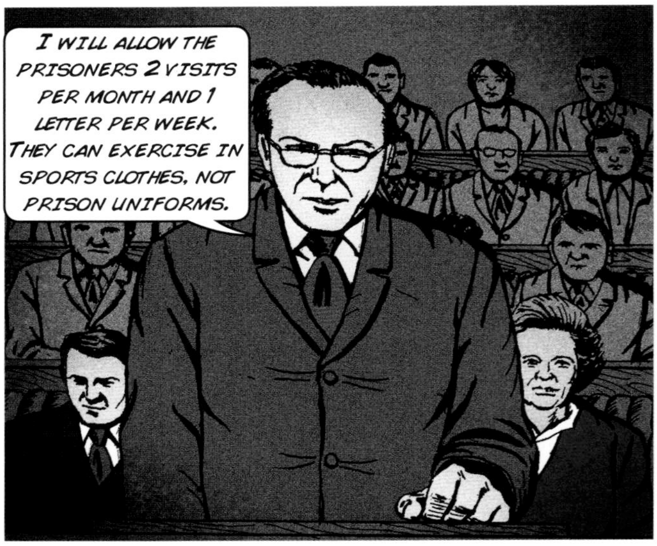
I WILL ALLOW THE PRISONERS 2 VISITS PER MONTH AND 1 LETTER PER WEEK. THEY CAN EXERCISE IN SPORTS CLOTHES, NOT PRISON UNIFORMS.

ON 26 MARCH 1980, HUMPHREY ATKINS MADE A SPECIAL ANNOUNCEMENT IN THE HOUSE OF COMMONS RE THE DEMANDS OF THE REPUBLICAN PRISONERS.

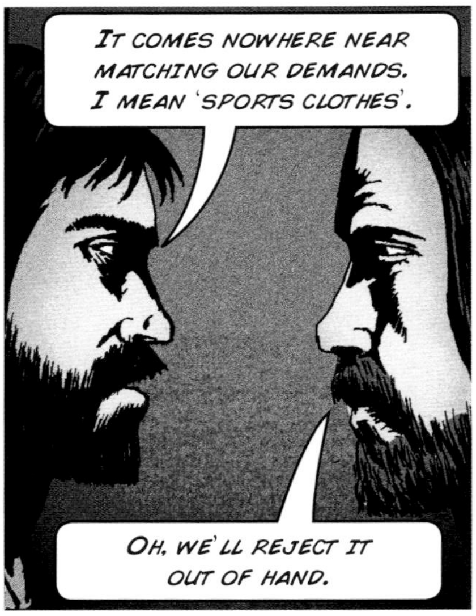
IT COMES NOWHERE NEAR MATCHING OUR DEMANDS. I MEAN 'SPORTS CLOTHES'.
OH, WE'LL REJECT IT OUT OF HAND.

HIS OFFER WAS DISCUSSED BY BRENDAN HUGHES AND BOBBY SANDS.

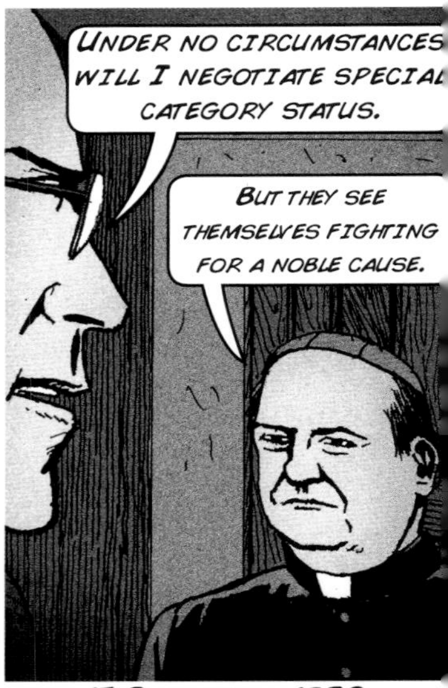
UNDER NO CIRCUMSTANCES WILL I NEGOTIATE SPECIAL CATEGORY STATUS.
BUT THEY SEE THEMSELVES FIGHTING FOR A NOBLE CAUSE.

17 SEPTEMBER 1980, CARDINAL Ó FIAICH DISCUSSED THE PRISONERS' REJECTION WITH ATKINS.

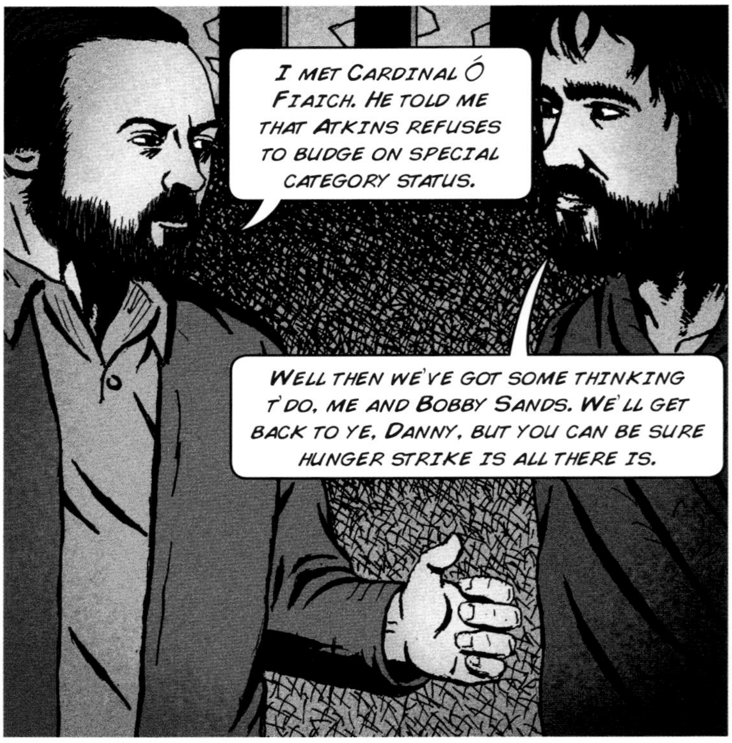
I MET CARDINAL Ó FIAICH. HE TOLD ME THAT ATKINS REFUSES TO BUDGE ON SPECIAL CATEGORY STATUS.
WELL THEN WE'VE GOT SOME THINKING T'DO, ME AND BOBBY SANDS. WE'LL GET BACK TO YE, DANNY, BUT YOU CAN BE SURE HUNGER STRIKE IS ALL THERE IS.

DANNY MORRISON WENT TO SEE BRENDAN HUGHES WITH THE LATEST NEWS.

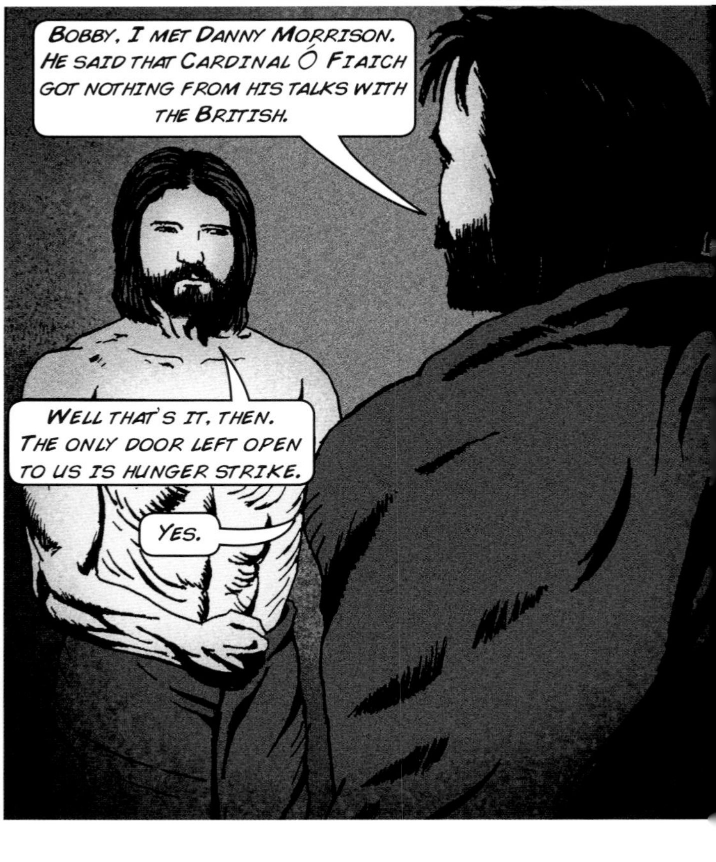
BOBBY, I MET DANNY MORRISON. HE SAID THAT CARDINAL Ó FIAICH GOT NOTHING FROM HIS TALKS WITH THE BRITISH.
WELL THAT'S IT, THEN. THE ONLY DOOR LEFT OPEN TO US IS HUNGER STRIKE.
YES.

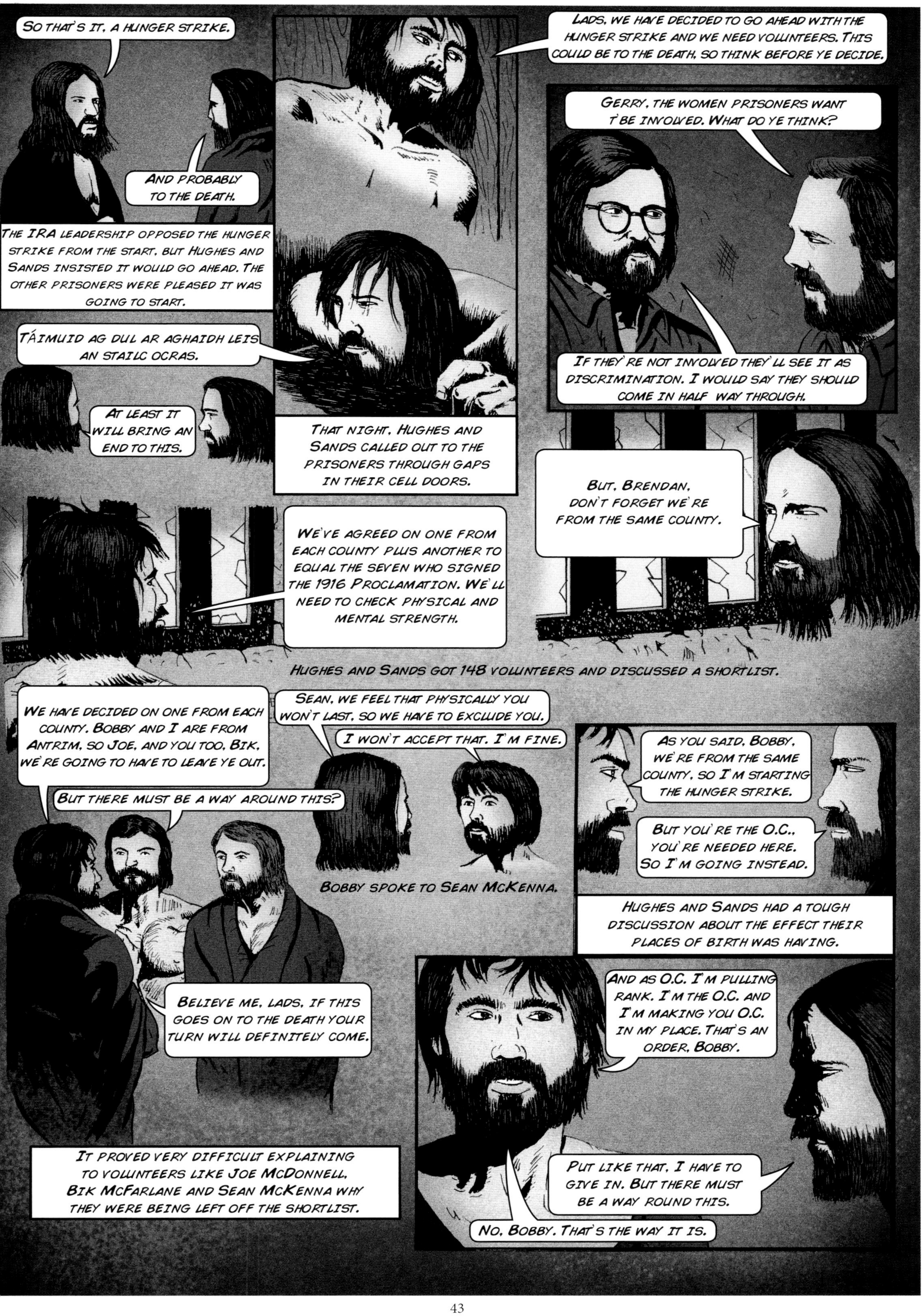
So that's it, a hunger strike.
And probably to the death.
The IRA leadership opposed the hunger strike from the start, but Hughes and Sands insisted it would go ahead. The other prisoners were pleased it was going to start.
Táimuid ag dul ar aghaidh leis an stailc ocras.
At least it will bring an end to this.
Lads, we have decided to go ahead with the hunger strike and we need volunteers. This could be to the death, so think before ye decide.
That night, Hughes and Sands called out to the prisoners through gaps in their cell doors.
Gerry, the women prisoners want t'be involved. What do ye think?
If they're not involved they'll see it as discrimination. I would say they should come in half way through.
We've agreed on one from each county plus another to equal the seven who signed the 1916 Proclamation. We'll need to check physical and mental strength.
But, Brendan, don't forget we're from the same county.
Hughes and Sands got 148 volunteers and discussed a shortlist.
We have decided on one from each county. Bobby and I are from Antrim, so Joe, and you too, Bik, we're going to have to leave ye out.
But there must be a way around this?
Sean, we feel that physically you won't last, so we have to exclude you.
I won't accept that. I'm fine.
Bobby spoke to Sean McKenna.
As you said, Bobby, we're from the same county, so I'm starting the hunger strike.
But you're the O.C., you're needed here. So I'm going instead.
Hughes and Sands had a tough discussion about the effect their places of birth was having.
Believe me, lads, if this goes on to the death your turn will definitely come.
And as O.C. I'm pulling rank. I'm the O.C. and I'm making you O.C. in my place. That's an order, Bobby.
It proved very difficult explaining to volunteers like Joe McDonnell, Bik McFarlane and Sean McKenna why they were being left off the shortlist.
Put like that, I have to give in. But there must be a way round this.
No, Bobby. That's the way it is.

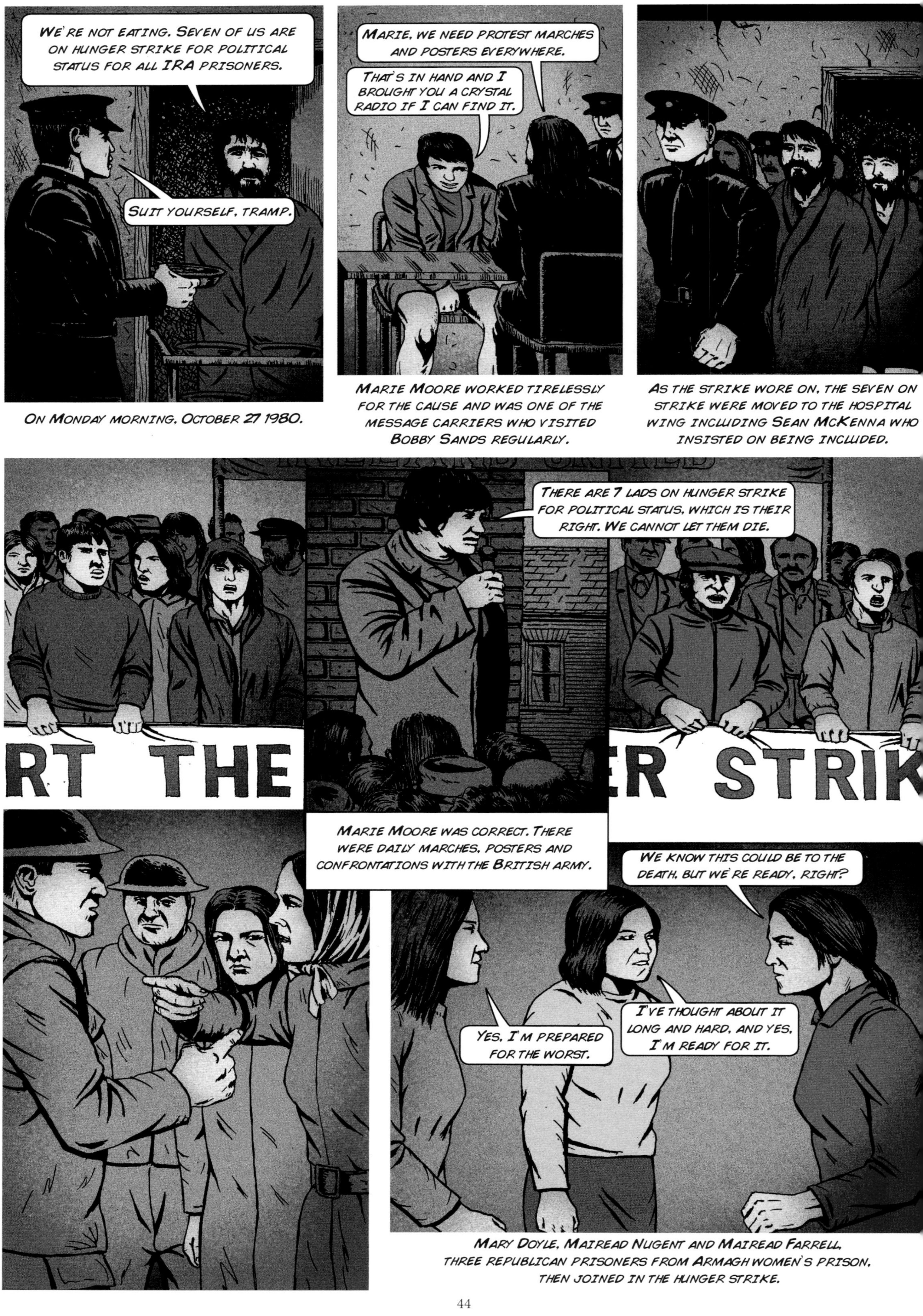
WE'RE NOT EATING. SEVEN OF US ARE ON HUNGER STRIKE FOR POLITICAL STATUS FOR ALL IRA PRISONERS.
SUIT YOURSELF, TRAMP.
ON MONDAY MORNING, OCTOBER 27 1980.
MARIE, WE NEED PROTEST MARCHES AND POSTERS EVERYWHERE.
THAT'S IN HAND AND I BROUGHT YOU A CRYSTAL RADIO IF I CAN FIND IT.
MARIE MOORE WORKED TIRELESSLY FOR THE CAUSE AND WAS ONE OF THE MESSAGE CARRIERS WHO VISITED BOBBY SANDS REGULARLY.
AS THE STRIKE WORE ON, THE SEVEN ON STRIKE WERE MOVED TO THE HOSPITAL WING INCLUDING SEAN McKENNA WHO INSISTED ON BEING INCLUDED.
THERE ARE 7 LADS ON HUNGER STRIKE FOR POLITICAL STATUS, WHICH IS THEIR RIGHT. WE CANNOT LET THEM DIE.
RT THE
ER STRIK
MARIE MOORE WAS CORRECT. THERE WERE DAILY MARCHES, POSTERS AND CONFRONTATIONS WITH THE BRITISH ARMY.
WE KNOW THIS COULD BE TO THE DEATH, BUT WE'RE READY, RIGHT?
YES, I'M PREPARED FOR THE WORST.
I'VE THOUGHT ABOUT IT LONG AND HARD, AND YES, I'M READY FOR IT.
MARY DOYLE, MAIREAD NUGENT AND MAIREAD FARRELL, THREE REPUBLICAN PRISONERS FROM ARMAGH WOMEN'S PRISON, THEN JOINED IN THE HUNGER STRIKE.

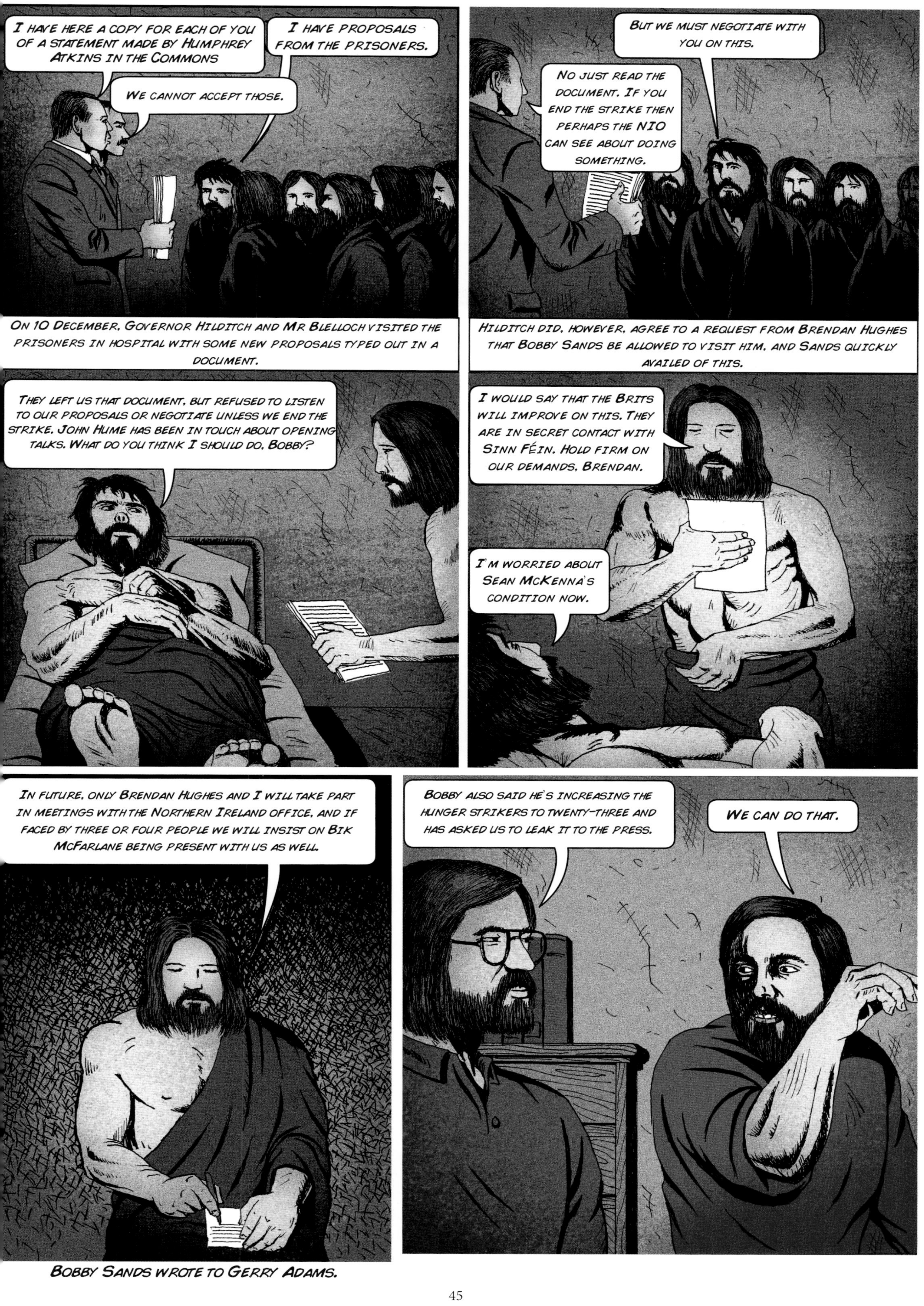
I HAVE HERE A COPY FOR EACH OF YOU OF A STATEMENT MADE BY HUMPHREY ATKINS IN THE COMMONS
I HAVE PROPOSALS FROM THE PRISONERS.
WE CANNOT ACCEPT THOSE.
ON 10 DECEMBER, GOVERNOR HILDITCH AND MR BLELLOCH VISITED THE PRISONERS IN HOSPITAL WITH SOME NEW PROPOSALS TYPED OUT IN A DOCUMENT.
BUT WE MUST NEGOTIATE WITH YOU ON THIS.
NO JUST READ THE DOCUMENT. IF YOU END THE STRIKE THEN PERHAPS THE NIO CAN SEE ABOUT DOING SOMETHING.
HILDITCH DID, HOWEVER, AGREE TO A REQUEST FROM BRENDAN HUGHES THAT BOBBY SANDS BE ALLOWED TO VISIT HIM, AND SANDS QUICKLY AVAILED OF THIS.
THEY LEFT US THAT DOCUMENT, BUT REFUSED TO LISTEN TO OUR PROPOSALS OR NEGOTIATE UNLESS WE END THE STRIKE. JOHN HUME HAS BEEN IN TOUCH ABOUT OPENING TALKS. WHAT DO YOU THINK I SHOULD DO, BOBBY?
I WOULD SAY THAT THE BRITS WILL IMPROVE ON THIS. THEY ARE IN SECRET CONTACT WITH SINN FÉIN. HOLD FIRM ON OUR DEMANDS, BRENDAN.
I'M WORRIED ABOUT SEAN MCKENNA'S CONDITION NOW.
IN FUTURE, ONLY BRENDAN HUGHES AND I WILL TAKE PART IN MEETINGS WITH THE NORTHERN IRELAND OFFICE, AND IF FACED BY THREE OR FOUR PEOPLE WE WILL INSIST ON BIK MCFARLANE BEING PRESENT WITH US AS WELL.
BOBBY ALSO SAID HE'S INCREASING THE HUNGER STRIKERS TO TWENTY-THREE AND HAS ASKED US TO LEAK IT TO THE PRESS.
WE CAN DO THAT.

BOBBY SANDS WROTE TO GERRY ADAMS.

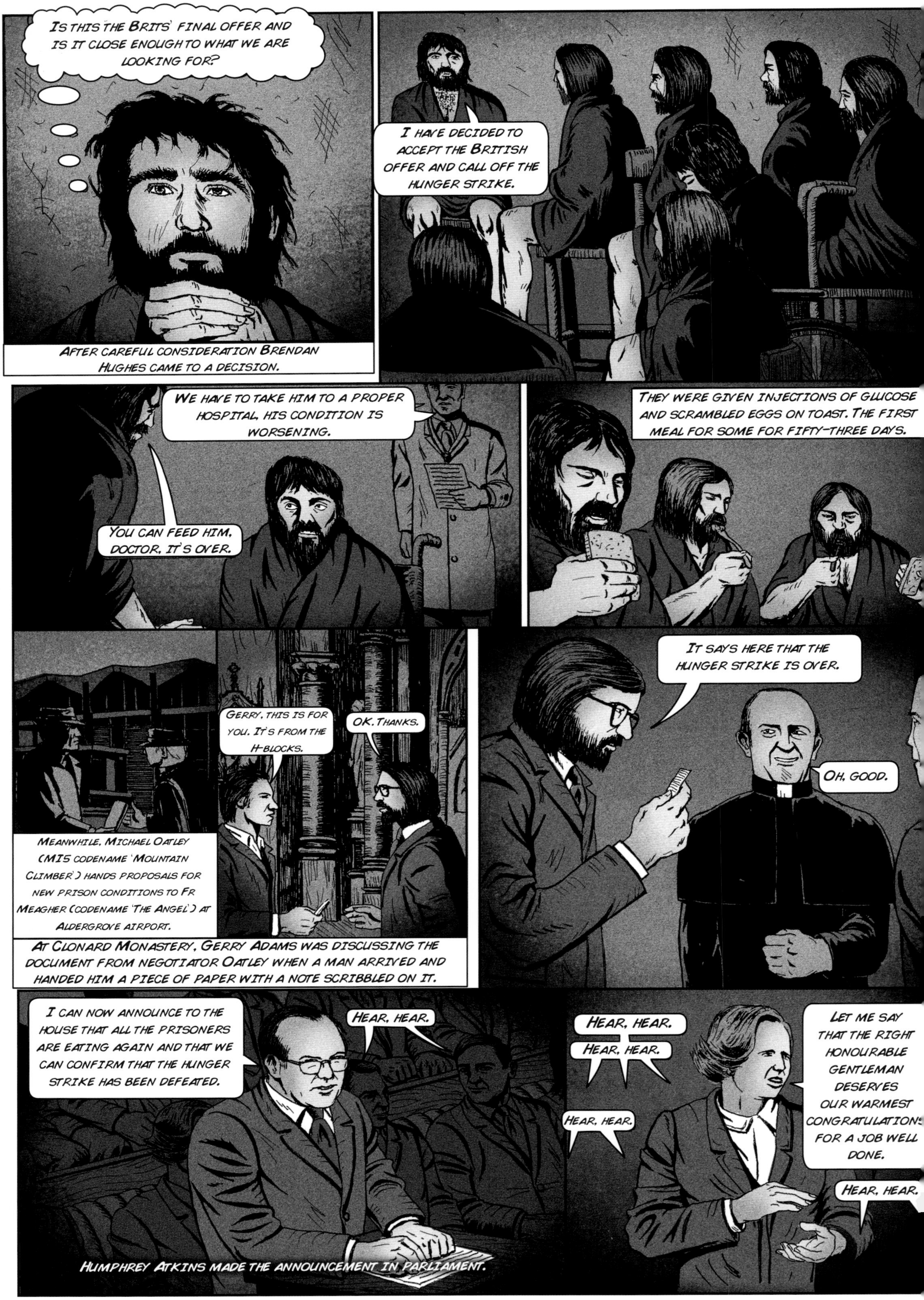

IS THIS THE BRITS' FINAL OFFER AND IS IT CLOSE ENOUGH TO WHAT WE ARE LOOKING FOR?
AFTER CAREFUL CONSIDERATION BRENDAN HUGHES CAME TO A DECISION.
I HAVE DECIDED TO ACCEPT THE BRITISH OFFER AND CALL OFF THE HUNGER STRIKE.
WE HAVE TO TAKE HIM TO A PROPER HOSPITAL, HIS CONDITION IS WORSENING.
YOU CAN FEED HIM, DOCTOR, IT'S OVER.
THEY WERE GIVEN INJECTIONS OF GLUCOSE AND SCRAMBLED EGGS ON TOAST. THE FIRST MEAL FOR SOME FOR FIFTY-THREE DAYS.
MEANWHILE, MICHAEL OATLEY (MI5 CODENAME 'MOUNTAIN CLIMBER') HANDS PROPOSALS FOR NEW PRISON CONDITIONS TO FR MEAGHER (CODENAME 'THE ANGEL') AT ALDERGROVE AIRPORT.
GERRY, THIS IS FOR YOU. IT'S FROM THE H-BLOCKS.
OK. THANKS.
AT CLONARD MONASTERY, GERRY ADAMS WAS DISCUSSING THE DOCUMENT FROM NEGOTIATOR OATLEY WHEN A MAN ARRIVED AND HANDED HIM A PIECE OF PAPER WITH A NOTE SCRIBBLED ON IT.
IT SAYS HERE THAT THE HUNGER STRIKE IS OVER.
OH, GOOD.
I CAN NOW ANNOUNCE TO THE HOUSE THAT ALL THE PRISONERS ARE EATING AGAIN AND THAT WE CAN CONFIRM THAT THE HUNGER STRIKE HAS BEEN DEFEATED.
HEAR, HEAR.
HEAR, HEAR.
HEAR, HEAR.
HEAR, HEAR.
LET ME SAY THAT THE RIGHT HONOURABLE GENTLEMAN DESERVES OUR WARMEST CONGRATULATIONS FOR A JOB WELL DONE.
HEAR, HEAR.
HUMPHREY ATKINS MADE THE ANNOUNCEMENT IN PARLIAMENT.

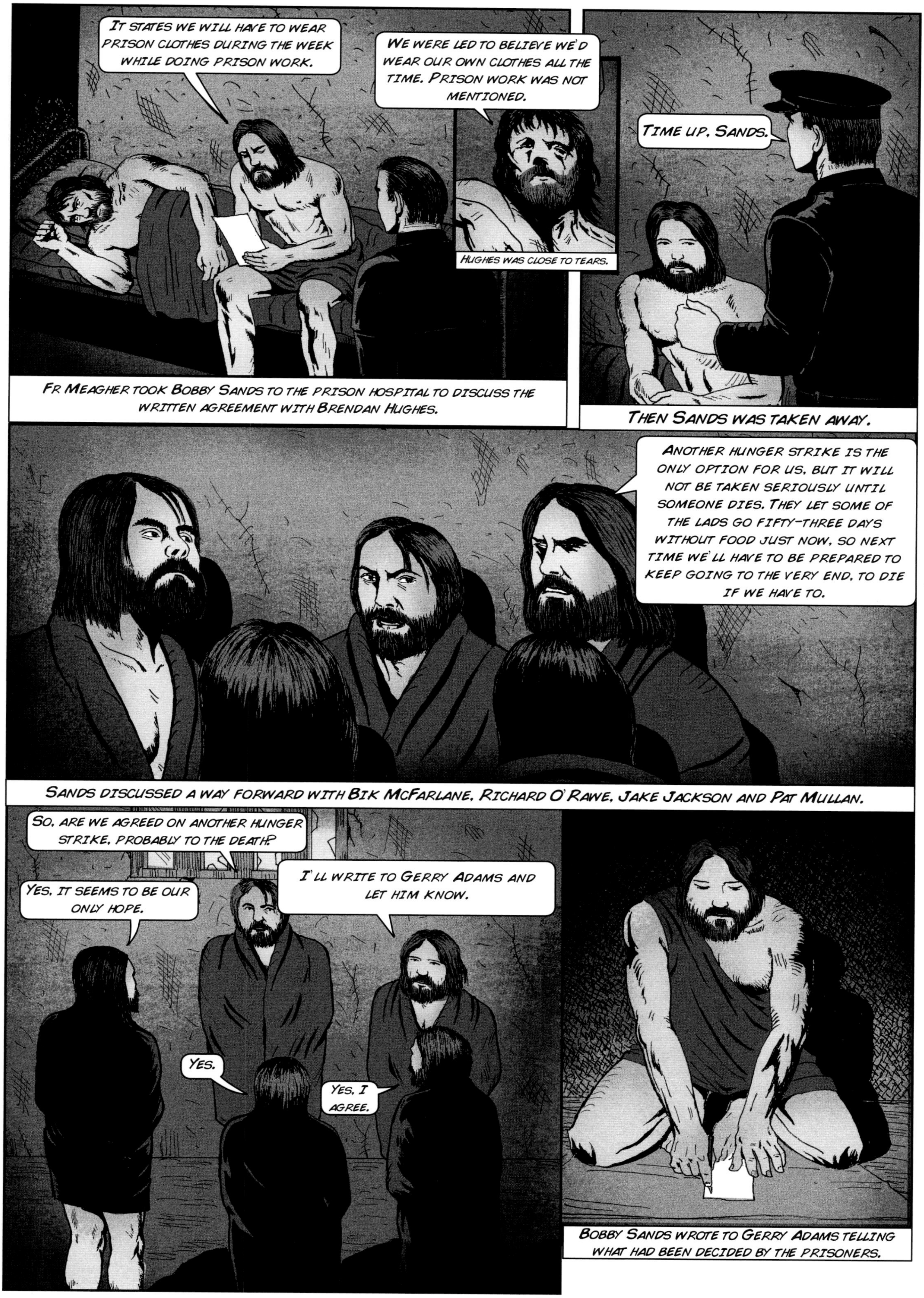

It states we will have to wear prison clothes during the week while doing prison work.
We were led to believe we'd wear our own clothes all the time. Prison work was not mentioned.
Hughes was close to tears.
Time up, Sands.
Fr Meagher took Bobby Sands to the prison hospital to discuss the written agreement with Brendan Hughes.
Then Sands was taken away.
Another hunger strike is the only option for us, but it will not be taken seriously until someone dies. They let some of the lads go fifty-three days without food just now, so next time we'll have to be prepared to keep going to the very end, to die if we have to.
Sands discussed a way forward with Bik McFarlane, Richard O'Rawe, Jake Jackson and Pat Mullan.
So, are we agreed on another hunger strike, probably to the death?
Yes, it seems to be our only hope.
I'll write to Gerry Adams and let him know.
Yes.
Yes, I agree.
Bobby Sands wrote to Gerry Adams telling what had been decided by the prisoners.

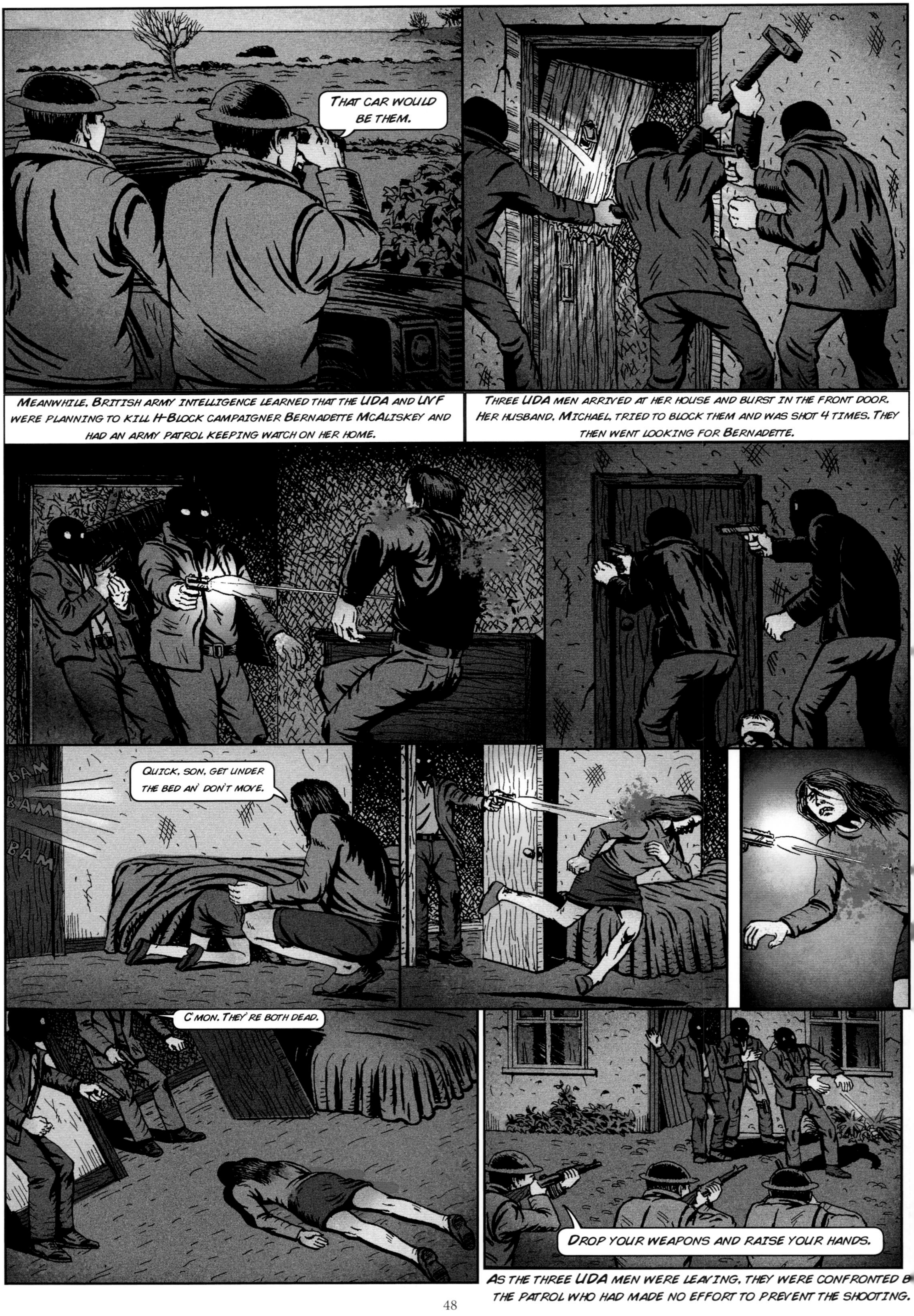
THAT CAR WOULD BE THEM.
MEANWHILE, BRITISH ARMY INTELLIGENCE LEARNED THAT THE UDA AND UVF WERE PLANNING TO KILL H-BLOCK CAMPAIGNER BERNADETTE MCALISKEY AND HAD AN ARMY PATROL KEEPING WATCH ON HER HOME.
THREE UDA MEN ARRIVED AT HER HOUSE AND BURST IN THE FRONT DOOR. HER HUSBAND, MICHAEL, TRIED TO BLOCK THEM AND WAS SHOT 4 TIMES. THEY THEN WENT LOOKING FOR BERNADETTE.
BAM
BAM
BAM
QUICK, SON, GET UNDER THE BED AN' DON'T MOVE.
C'MON. THEY'RE BOTH DEAD.
DROP YOUR WEAPONS AND RAISE YOUR HANDS.
AS THE THREE UDA MEN WERE LEAVING, THEY WERE CONFRONTED B
THE PATROL WHO HAD MADE NO EFFORT TO PREVENT THE SHOOTING.

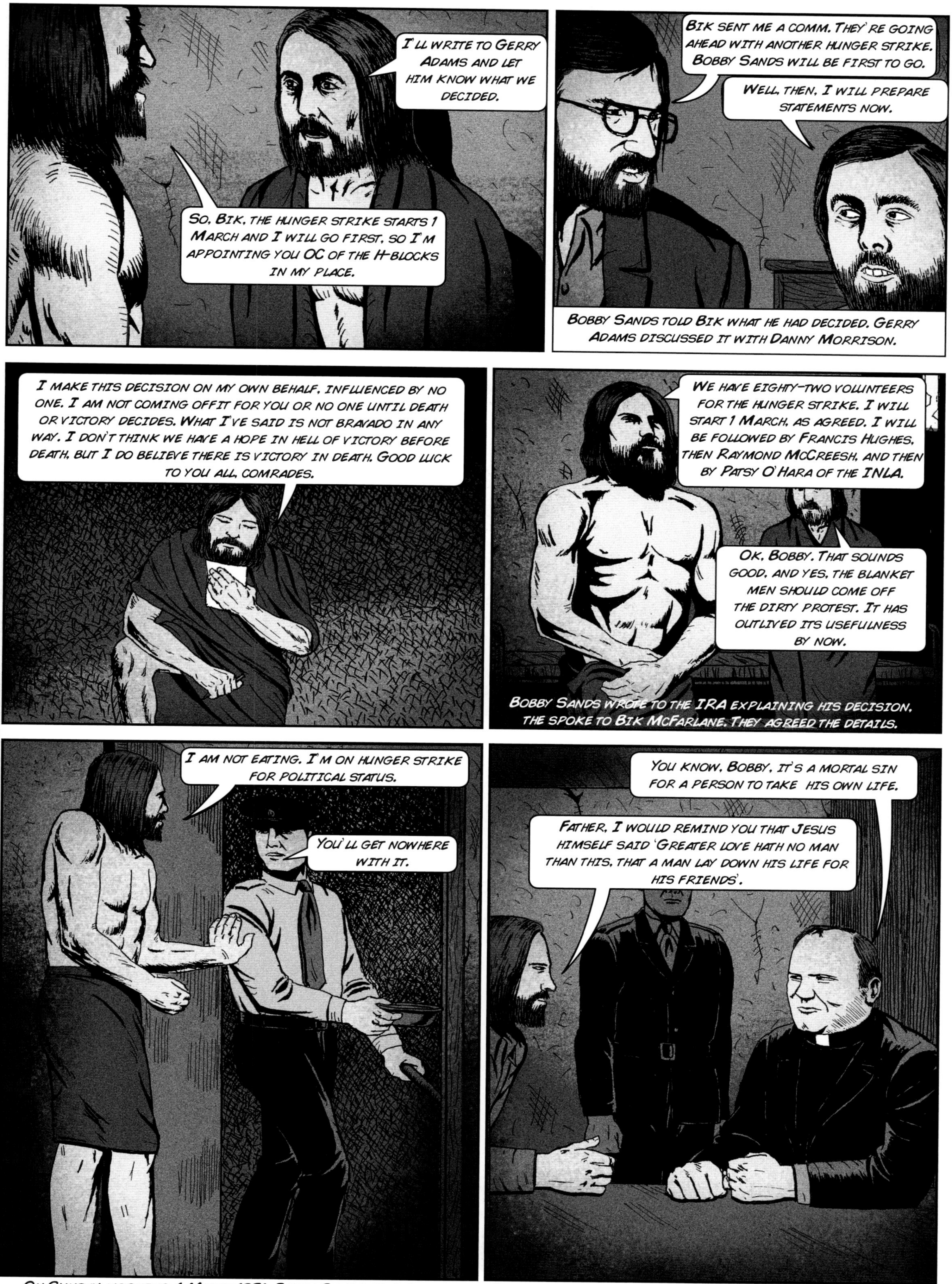
I'll write to Gerry Adams and let him know what we decided.
So, Bik, the hunger strike starts 1 March and I will go first, so I'm appointing you OC of the H-blocks in my place.
Bik sent me a comm. They're going ahead with another hunger strike. Bobby Sands will be first to go.
Well, then, I will prepare statements now.
Bobby Sands told Bik what he had decided. Gerry Adams discussed it with Danny Morrison.
I make this decision on my own behalf, influenced by no one. I am not coming off it for you or no one until death or victory decides. What I've said is not bravado in any way. I don't think we have a hope in hell of victory before death, but I do believe there is victory in death. Good luck to you all, comrades.
We have eighty-two volunteers for the hunger strike. I will start 1 March, as agreed. I will be followed by Francis Hughes, then Raymond McCreesh, and then by Patsy O'Hara of the INLA.
OK, Bobby. That sounds good, and yes, the blanket men should come off the dirty protest. It has outlived its usefulness by now.
Bobby Sands wrote to the IRA explaining his decision, the spoke to Bik McFarlane. They agreed the details.
I am not eating. I'm on hunger strike for political status.
You'll get nowhere with it.
You know, Bobby, it's a mortal sin for a person to take his own life.
Father, I would remind you that Jesus himself said 'Greater love hath no man than this, that a man lay down his life for his friends'.

On Sunday morning, 1 March 1981, Bobby Sands started the second hunger strike by refusing to eat his breakfast.

He was visited by Fr. Denis Faul who made a futile attempt to persuade him to give up the hunger strike.

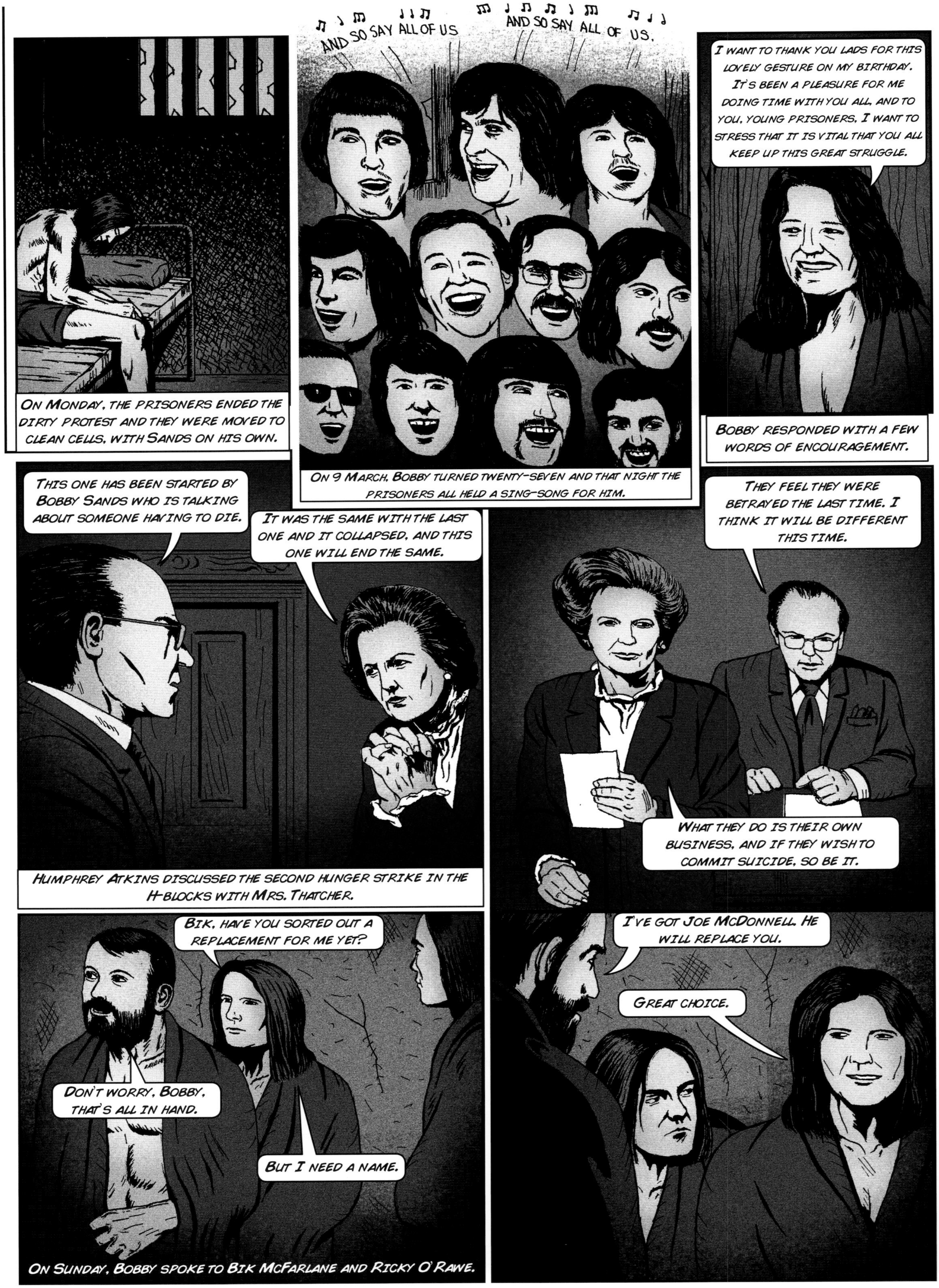
On Monday, the prisoners ended the dirty protest and they were moved to clean cells, with Sands on his own.
And so say all of us
And so say all of us.
On 9 March, Bobby turned twenty-seven and that night the prisoners all held a sing-song for him.
I want to thank you lads for this lovely gesture on my birthday. It's been a pleasure for me doing time with you all, and to you, young prisoners, I want to stress that it is vital that you all keep up this great struggle.
Bobby responded with a few words of encouragement.
This one has been started by Bobby Sands who is talking about someone having to die.
It was the same with the last one and it collapsed, and this one will end the same.
Humphrey Atkins discussed the second hunger strike in the H-blocks with Mrs. Thatcher.
They feel they were betrayed the last time. I think it will be different this time.
What they do is their own business, and if they wish to commit suicide, so be it.
Bik, have you sorted out a replacement for me yet?
Don't worry, Bobby, that's all in hand.
But I need a name.
On Sunday, Bobby spoke to Bik McFarlane and Ricky O'Rawe.
I've got Joe McDonnell. He will replace you.
Great choice.

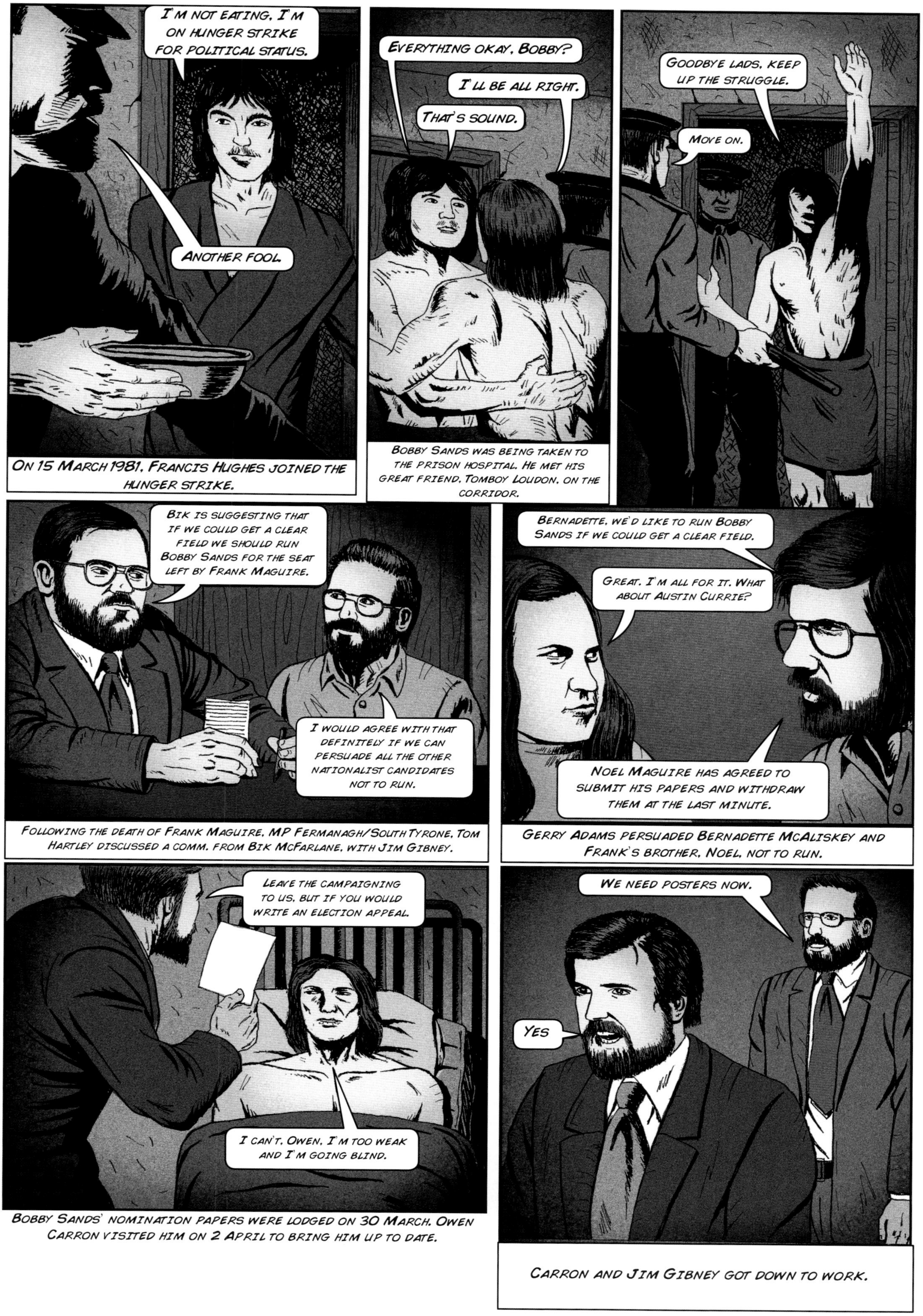
I'M NOT EATING. I'M ON HUNGER STRIKE FOR POLITICAL STATUS.
ANOTHER FOOL.
ON 15 MARCH 1981, FRANCIS HUGHES JOINED THE HUNGER STRIKE.
EVERYTHING OKAY, BOBBY?
I'LL BE ALL RIGHT.
THAT'S SOUND.
BOBBY SANDS WAS BEING TAKEN TO THE PRISON HOSPITAL. HE MET HIS GREAT FRIEND, TOMBOY LOUDON, ON THE CORRIDOR.
GOODBYE LADS, KEEP UP THE STRUGGLE.
MOVE ON.
BIK IS SUGGESTING THAT IF WE COULD GET A CLEAR FIELD WE SHOULD RUN BOBBY SANDS FOR THE SEAT LEFT BY FRANK MAGUIRE.
I WOULD AGREE WITH THAT DEFINITELY IF WE CAN PERSUADE ALL THE OTHER NATIONALIST CANDIDATES NOT TO RUN.
FOLLOWING THE DEATH OF FRANK MAGUIRE, MP FERMANAGH/SOUTH TYRONE, TOM HARTLEY DISCUSSED A COMM. FROM BIK MCFARLANE, WITH JIM GIBNEY.
BERNADETTE, WE'D LIKE TO RUN BOBBY SANDS IF WE COULD GET A CLEAR FIELD.
GREAT. I'M ALL FOR IT. WHAT ABOUT AUSTIN CURRIE?
NOEL MAGUIRE HAS AGREED TO SUBMIT HIS PAPERS AND WITHDRAW THEM AT THE LAST MINUTE.
GERRY ADAMS PERSUADED BERNADETTE MCALISKEY AND FRANK'S BROTHER, NOEL, NOT TO RUN.
LEAVE THE CAMPAIGNING TO US, BUT IF YOU WOULD WRITE AN ELECTION APPEAL.
I CAN'T, OWEN, I'M TOO WEAK AND I'M GOING BLIND.
BOBBY SANDS' NOMINATION PAPERS WERE LODGED ON 30 MARCH. OWEN CARRON VISITED HIM ON 2 APRIL TO BRING HIM UP TO DATE.
WE NEED POSTERS NOW.
YES
CARRON AND JIM GIBNEY GOT DOWN TO WORK.

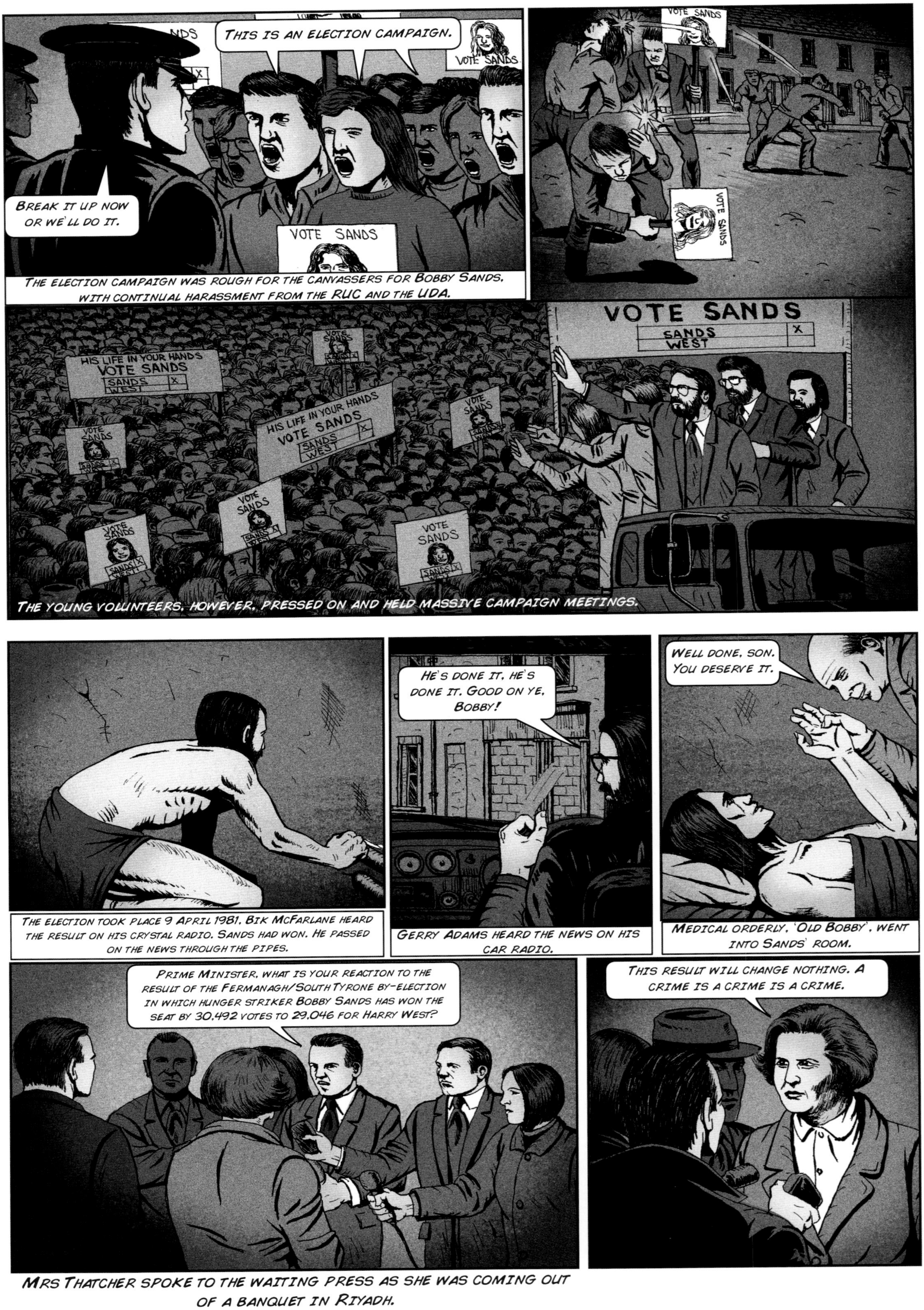
THIS IS AN ELECTION CAMPAIGN.
BREAK IT UP NOW OR WE'LL DO IT.
VOTE SANDS
VOTE SANDS
THE ELECTION CAMPAIGN WAS ROUGH FOR THE CANVASSERS FOR BOBBY SANDS, WITH CONTINUAL HARASSMENT FROM THE RUC AND THE UDA.
VOTE SANDS
VOTE SANDS
VOTE SANDS
SANDS X
WEST
HIS LIFE IN YOUR HANDS
VOTE SANDS
SANDS X
WEST
HIS LIFE IN YOUR HANDS
VOTE SANDS
SANDS X
WEST
THE YOUNG VOLUNTEERS, HOWEVER, PRESSED ON AND HELD MASSIVE CAMPAIGN MEETINGS.
THE ELECTION TOOK PLACE 9 APRIL 1981. BIK MCFARLANE HEARD THE RESULT ON HIS CRYSTAL RADIO. SANDS HAD WON. HE PASSED ON THE NEWS THROUGH THE PIPES.
HE'S DONE IT, HE'S DONE IT. GOOD ON YE, BOBBY!
GERRY ADAMS HEARD THE NEWS ON HIS CAR RADIO.
WELL DONE, SON. YOU DESERVE IT.
MEDICAL ORDERLY, 'OLD BOBBY', WENT INTO SANDS' ROOM.
PRIME MINISTER, WHAT IS YOUR REACTION TO THE RESULT OF THE FERMANAGH/SOUTH TYRONE BY-ELECTION IN WHICH HUNGER STRIKER BOBBY SANDS HAS WON THE SEAT BY 30,492 VOTES TO 29,046 FOR HARRY WEST?
THIS RESULT WILL CHANGE NOTHING. A CRIME IS A CRIME IS A CRIME.
MRS THATCHER SPOKE TO THE WAITING PRESS AS SHE WAS COMING OUT OF A BANQUET IN RIYADH.

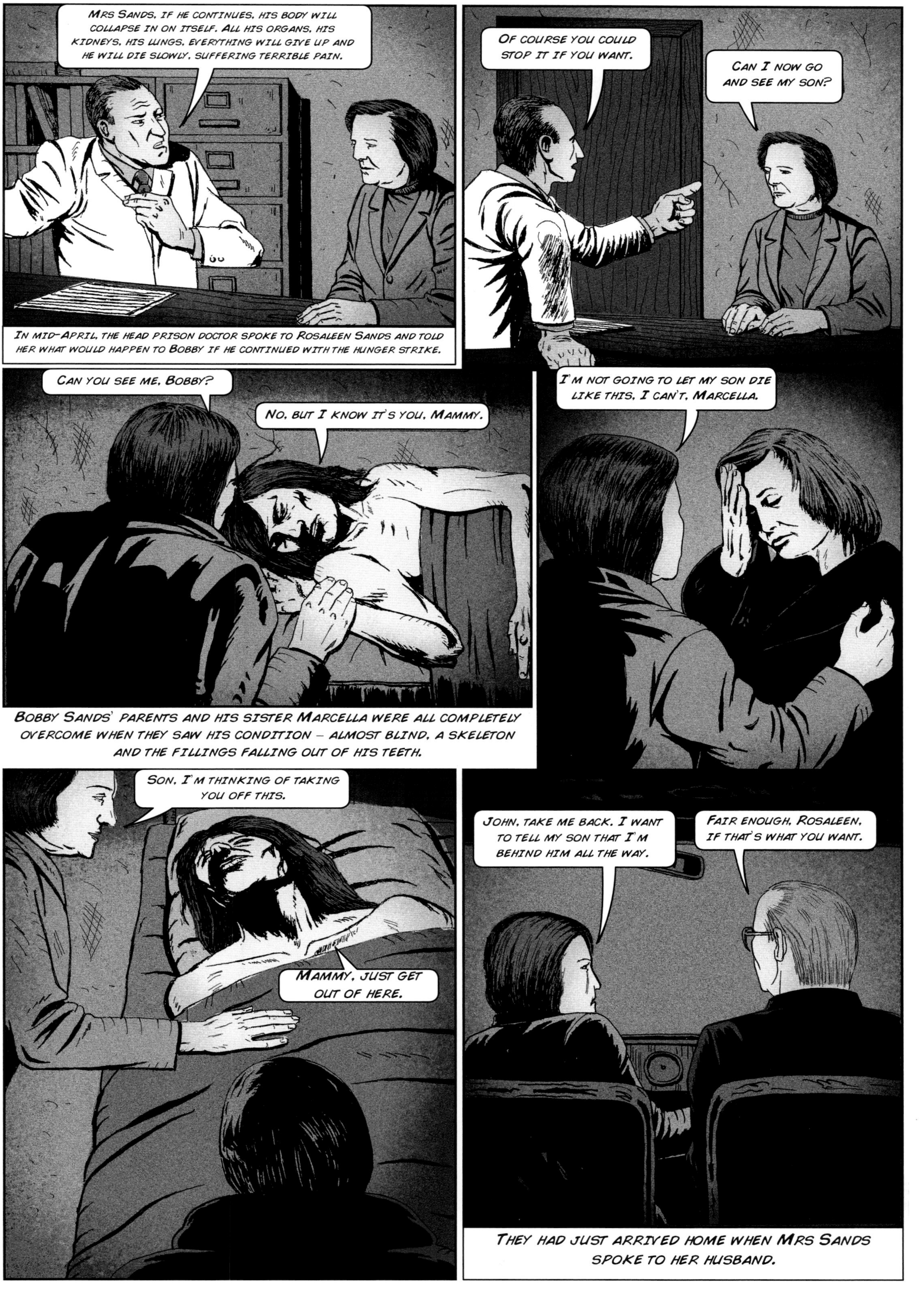

MRS SANDS, IF HE CONTINUES, HIS BODY WILL COLLAPSE IN ON ITSELF. ALL HIS ORGANS, HIS KIDNEYS, HIS LUNGS, EVERYTHING WILL GIVE UP AND HE WILL DIE SLOWLY, SUFFERING TERRIBLE PAIN.
IN MID-APRIL, THE HEAD PRISON DOCTOR SPOKE TO ROSALEEN SANDS AND TOLD HER WHAT WOULD HAPPEN TO BOBBY IF HE CONTINUED WITH THE HUNGER STRIKE.
OF COURSE YOU COULD STOP IT IF YOU WANT.
CAN I NOW GO AND SEE MY SON?
CAN YOU SEE ME, BOBBY?
NO, BUT I KNOW IT'S YOU, MAMMY.
BOBBY SANDS' PARENTS AND HIS SISTER MARCELLA WERE ALL COMPLETELY OVERCOME WHEN THEY SAW HIS CONDITION – ALMOST BLIND, A SKELETON AND THE FILLINGS FALLING OUT OF HIS TEETH.
I'M NOT GOING TO LET MY SON DIE LIKE THIS. I CAN'T, MARCELLA.
SON, I'M THINKING OF TAKING YOU OFF THIS.
MAMMY, JUST GET OUT OF HERE.
JOHN, TAKE ME BACK. I WANT TO TELL MY SON THAT I'M BEHIND HIM ALL THE WAY.
FAIR ENOUGH, ROSALEEN, IF THAT'S WHAT YOU WANT.
THEY HAD JUST ARRIVED HOME WHEN MRS SANDS SPOKE TO HER HUSBAND.

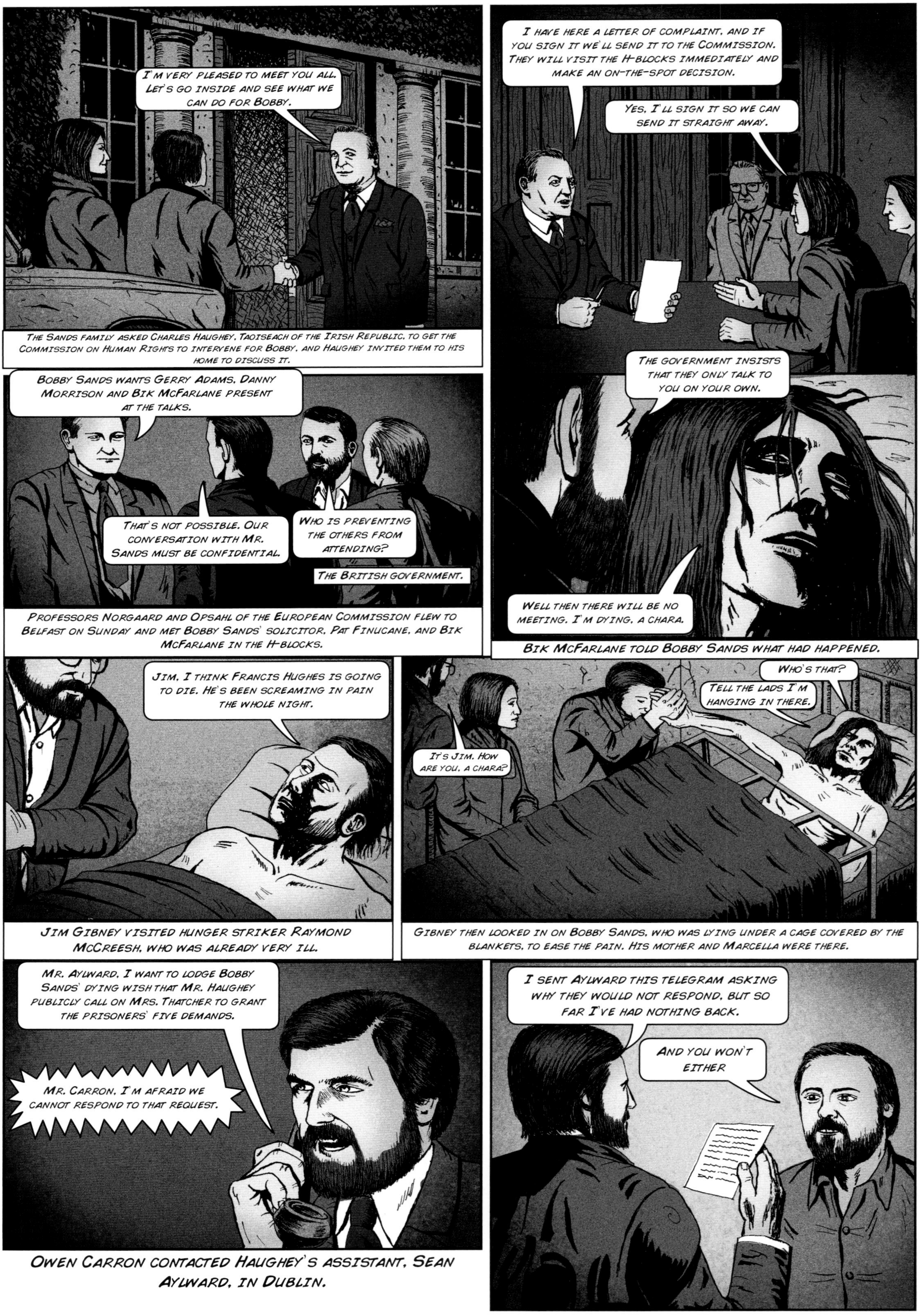
I'M VERY PLEASED TO MEET YOU ALL. LET'S GO INSIDE AND SEE WHAT WE CAN DO FOR BOBBY.
THE SANDS FAMILY ASKED CHARLES HAUGHEY, TAOISEACH OF THE IRISH REPUBLIC, TO GET THE COMMISSION ON HUMAN RIGHTS TO INTERVENE FOR BOBBY, AND HAUGHEY INVITED THEM TO HIS HOME TO DISCUSS IT.
I HAVE HERE A LETTER OF COMPLAINT, AND IF YOU SIGN IT WE'LL SEND IT TO THE COMMISSION. THEY WILL VISIT THE H-BLOCKS IMMEDIATELY AND MAKE AN ON-THE-SPOT DECISION.
YES, I'LL SIGN IT SO WE CAN SEND IT STRAIGHT AWAY.
BOBBY SANDS WANTS GERRY ADAMS, DANNY MORRISON AND BIK MCFARLANE PRESENT AT THE TALKS.
THAT'S NOT POSSIBLE. OUR CONVERSATION WITH MR. SANDS MUST BE CONFIDENTIAL.
WHO IS PREVENTING THE OTHERS FROM ATTENDING?
THE BRITISH GOVERNMENT.
PROFESSORS NORGAARD AND OPSAHL OF THE EUROPEAN COMMISSION FLEW TO BELFAST ON SUNDAY AND MET BOBBY SANDS' SOLICITOR, PAT FINUCANE, AND BIK MCFARLANE IN THE H-BLOCKS.
THE GOVERNMENT INSISTS THAT THEY ONLY TALK TO YOU ON YOUR OWN.
WELL THEN THERE WILL BE NO MEETING. I'M DYING, A CHARA.
BIK MCFARLANE TOLD BOBBY SANDS WHAT HAD HAPPENED.
JIM, I THINK FRANCIS HUGHES IS GOING TO DIE. HE'S BEEN SCREAMING IN PAIN THE WHOLE NIGHT.
JIM GIBNEY VISITED HUNGER STRIKER RAYMOND MCCREESH, WHO WAS ALREADY VERY ILL.
WHO'S THAT?
IT'S JIM. HOW ARE YOU, A CHARA?
TELL THE LADS I'M HANGING IN THERE.
GIBNEY THEN LOOKED IN ON BOBBY SANDS, WHO WAS LYING UNDER A CAGE COVERED BY THE BLANKETS, TO EASE THE PAIN. HIS MOTHER AND MARCELLA WERE THERE.
MR. AYLWARD, I WANT TO LODGE BOBBY SANDS' DYING WISH THAT MR. HAUGHEY PUBLICLY CALL ON MRS. THATCHER TO GRANT THE PRISONERS' FIVE DEMANDS.
MR. CARRON, I'M AFRAID WE CANNOT RESPOND TO THAT REQUEST.
OWEN CARRON CONTACTED HAUGHEY'S ASSISTANT, SEAN AYLWARD, IN DUBLIN.
I SENT AYLWARD THIS TELEGRAM ASKING WHY THEY WOULD NOT RESPOND, BUT SO FAR I'VE HAD NOTHING BACK.
AND YOU WON'T EITHER

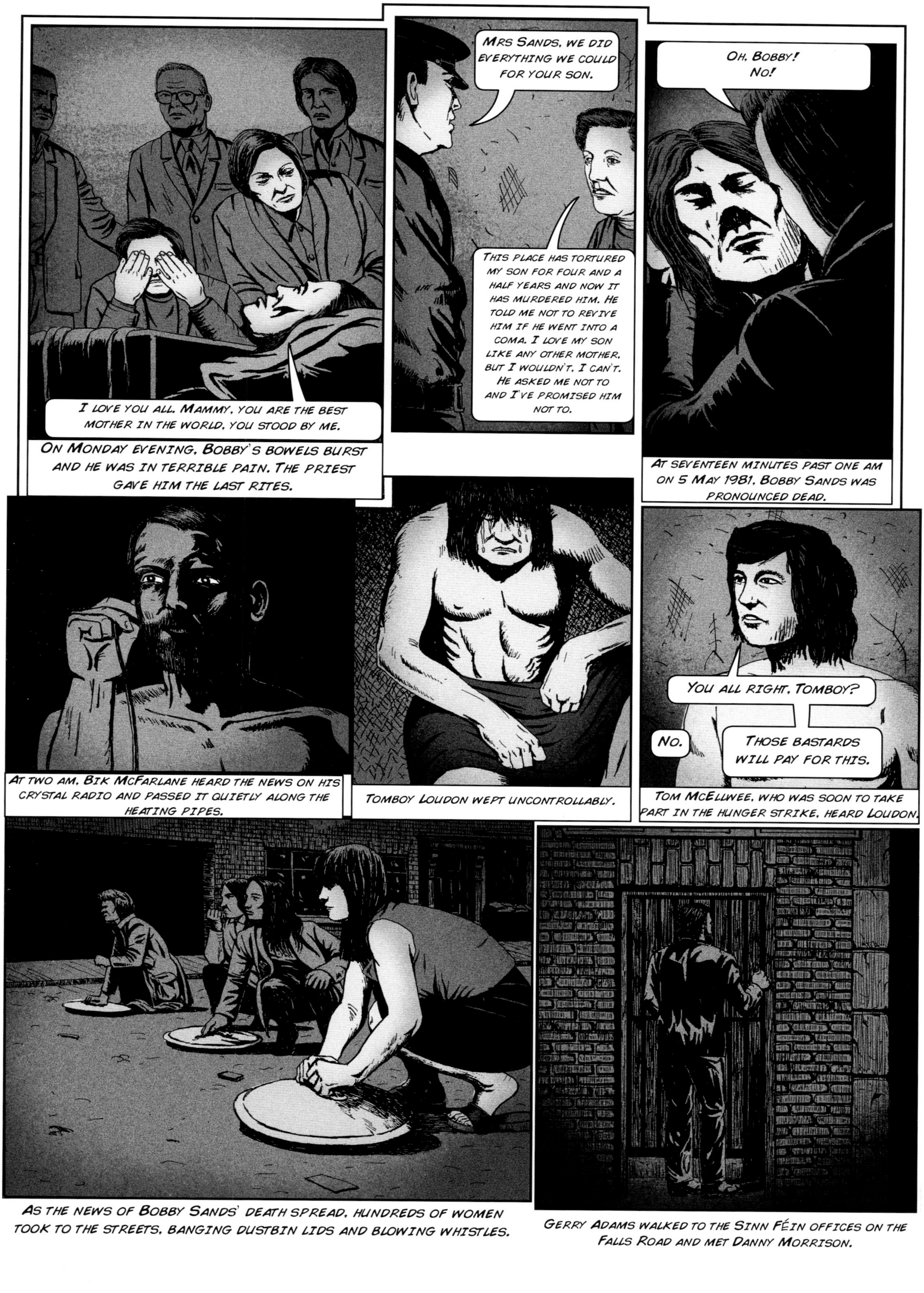
I LOVE YOU ALL. MAMMY, YOU ARE THE BEST MOTHER IN THE WORLD, YOU STOOD BY ME.
ON MONDAY EVENING, BOBBY'S BOWELS BURST AND HE WAS IN TERRIBLE PAIN. THE PRIEST GAVE HIM THE LAST RITES.
MRS SANDS, WE DID EVERYTHING WE COULD FOR YOUR SON.
THIS PLACE HAS TORTURED MY SON FOR FOUR AND A HALF YEARS AND NOW IT HAS MURDERED HIM. HE TOLD ME NOT TO REVIVE HIM IF HE WENT INTO A COMA. I LOVE MY SON LIKE ANY OTHER MOTHER, BUT I WOULDN'T. I CAN'T. HE ASKED ME NOT TO AND I'VE PROMISED HIM NOT TO.
OH, BOBBY! NO!
AT SEVENTEEN MINUTES PAST ONE AM ON 5 MAY 1981, BOBBY SANDS WAS PRONOUNCED DEAD.
AT TWO AM, BIK MCFARLANE HEARD THE NEWS ON HIS CRYSTAL RADIO AND PASSED IT QUIETLY ALONG THE HEATING PIPES.
TOMBOY LOUDON WEPT UNCONTROLLABLY.
YOU ALL RIGHT, TOMBOY?
NO.
THOSE BASTARDS WILL PAY FOR THIS.
TOM MCELLWEE, WHO WAS SOON TO TAKE PART IN THE HUNGER STRIKE, HEARD LOUDON.
AS THE NEWS OF BOBBY SANDS' DEATH SPREAD, HUNDREDS OF WOMEN TOOK TO THE STREETS, BANGING DUSTBIN LIDS AND BLOWING WHISTLES.
GERRY ADAMS WALKED TO THE SINN FÉIN OFFICES ON THE FALLS ROAD AND MET DANNY MORRISON.

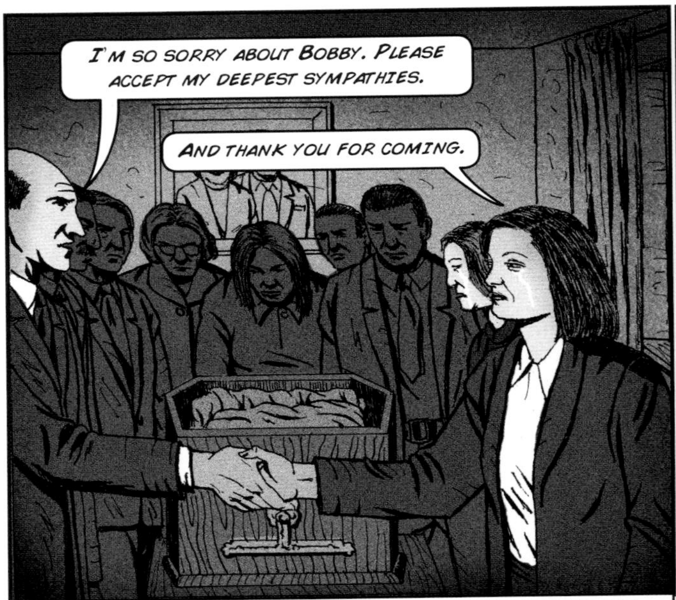
I'M SO SORRY ABOUT BOBBY. PLEASE ACCEPT MY DEEPEST SYMPATHIES.
AND THANK YOU FOR COMING.

THE REMAINS WERE MOVED TO HIS HOME IN TWINBROOK AND MARCELLA STOOD BY HIS COFFIN FOR HOURS, GREETING PEOPLE.

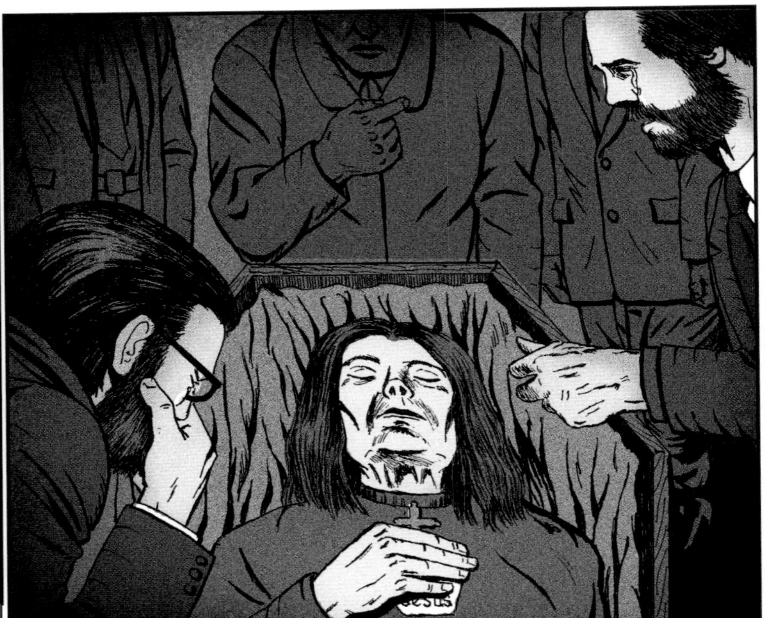

DANNY MORRISON AND JIM GIBNEY BROKE DOWN.

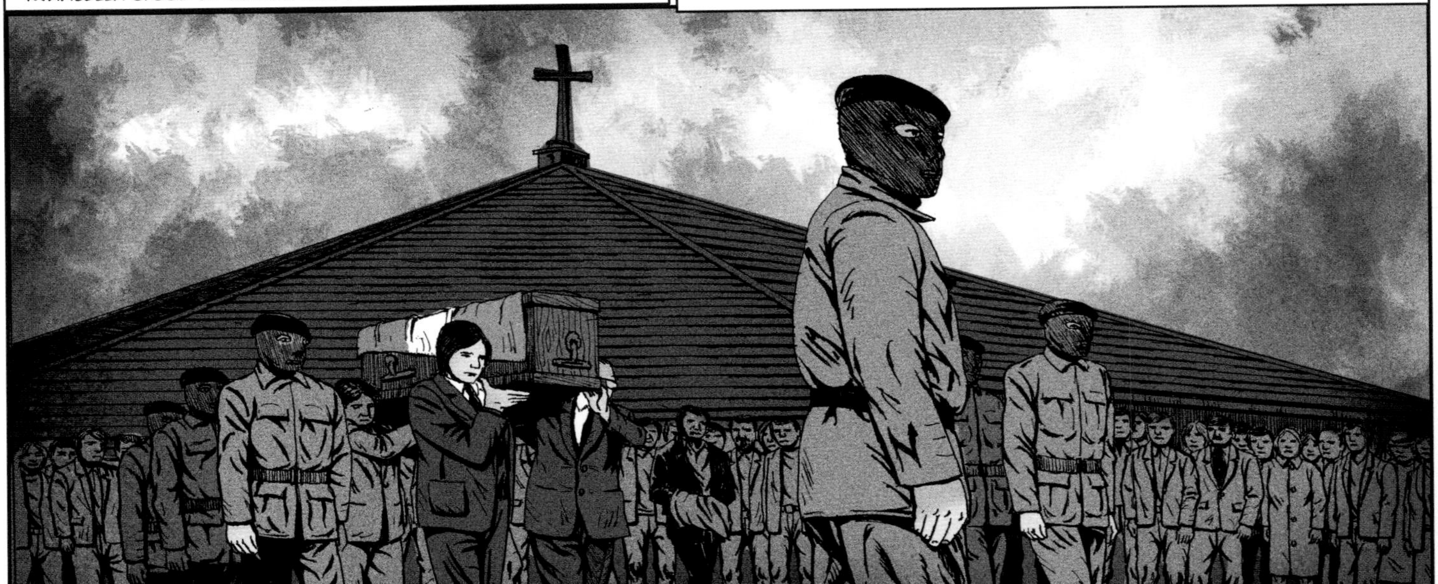

TENS OF THOUSANDS LINED THE ROAD FROM THE FAMILY HOME TO ST. LUKE'S CHAPEL. THERE WERE CAMERA CREWS FROM ALL OVER THE WORLD. BEFORE BEING ALLOWED INTO THE CHAPEL, THE TRICOLOR, GLOVES AND BLACK BERET HAD TO BE REMOVED FROM THE COFFIN. THE UNION JACK WOULD HAVE BEEN ALLOWED.

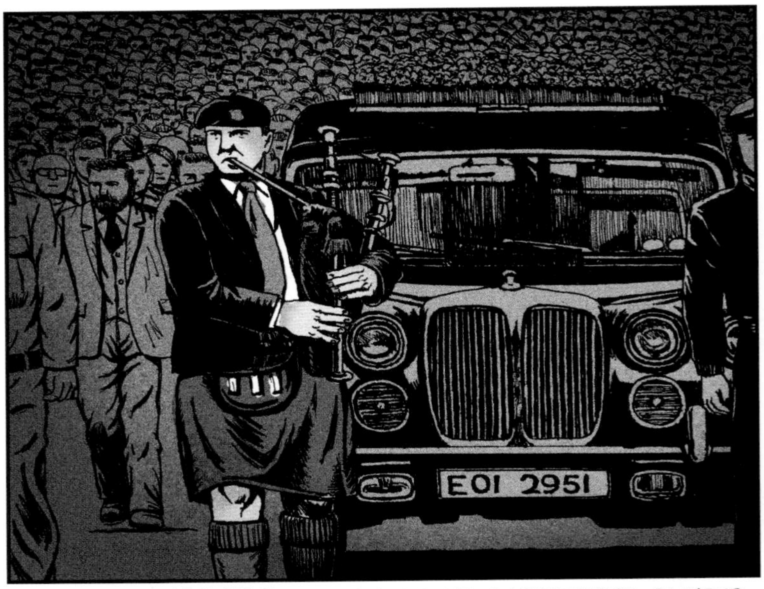
EOI 2951

A CROWD OF 100,000 PEOPLE FOLLOWED A LONE PIPER, PLAYING THE H-BLOCKS SONG, TO MILLTOWN CEMETERY.

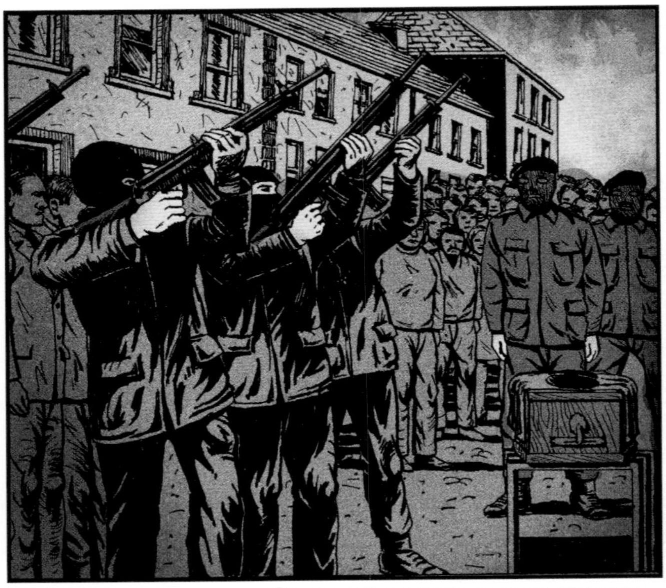

AT ANDERSONSTOWN ROAD, THE COFFIN WAS PLACED ON TRESTLES AND THREE VOLLEYS WERE FIRED. A MINUTE'S SILENCE FOLLOWED.

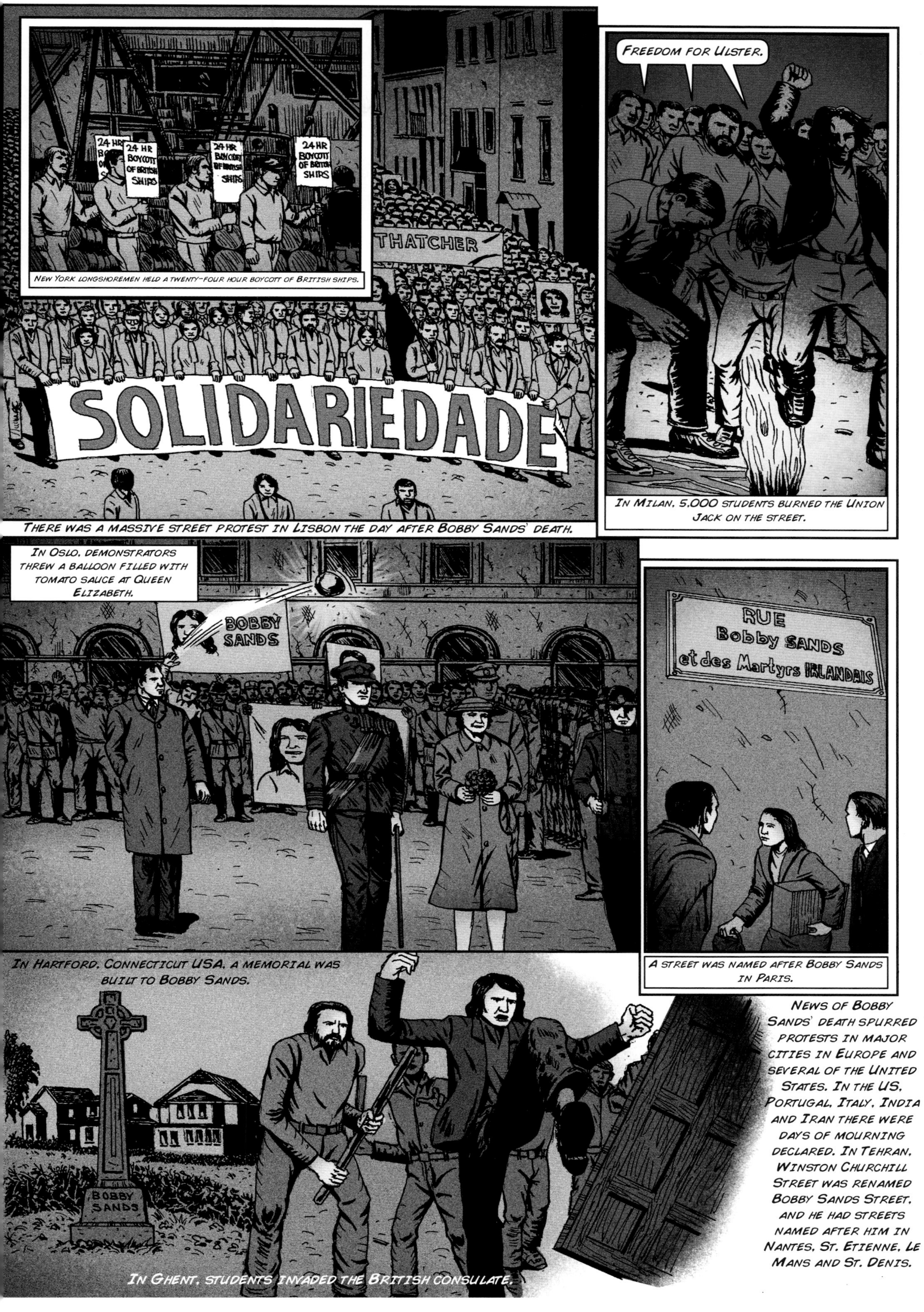
24 HR BOYCOTT OF BRITISH SHIPS
NEW YORK LONGSHOREMEN HELD A TWENTY-FOUR HOUR BOYCOTT OF BRITISH SHIPS.
THATCHER
SOLIDARIEDADE
THERE WAS A MASSIVE STREET PROTEST IN LISBON THE DAY AFTER BOBBY SANDS' DEATH.
FREEDOM FOR ULSTER.
IN MILAN, 5,000 STUDENTS BURNED THE UNION JACK ON THE STREET.
IN OSLO, DEMONSTRATORS THREW A BALLOON FILLED WITH TOMATO SAUCE AT QUEEN ELIZABETH.
BOBBY SANDS
RUE Bobby SANDS et des Martyrs IRLANDAIS
A STREET WAS NAMED AFTER BOBBY SANDS IN PARIS.
IN HARTFORD, CONNECTICUT USA, A MEMORIAL WAS BUILT TO BOBBY SANDS.
BOBBY SANDS
NEWS OF BOBBY SANDS' DEATH SPURRED PROTESTS IN MAJOR CITIES IN EUROPE AND SEVERAL OF THE UNITED STATES. IN THE US, PORTUGAL, ITALY, INDIA AND IRAN THERE WERE DAYS OF MOURNING DECLARED. IN TEHRAN, WINSTON CHURCHILL STREET WAS RENAMED BOBBY SANDS STREET, AND HE HAD STREETS NAMED AFTER HIM IN NANTES, ST. ETIENNE, LE MANS AND ST. DENIS.
IN GHENT, STUDENTS INVADED THE BRITISH CONSULATE.

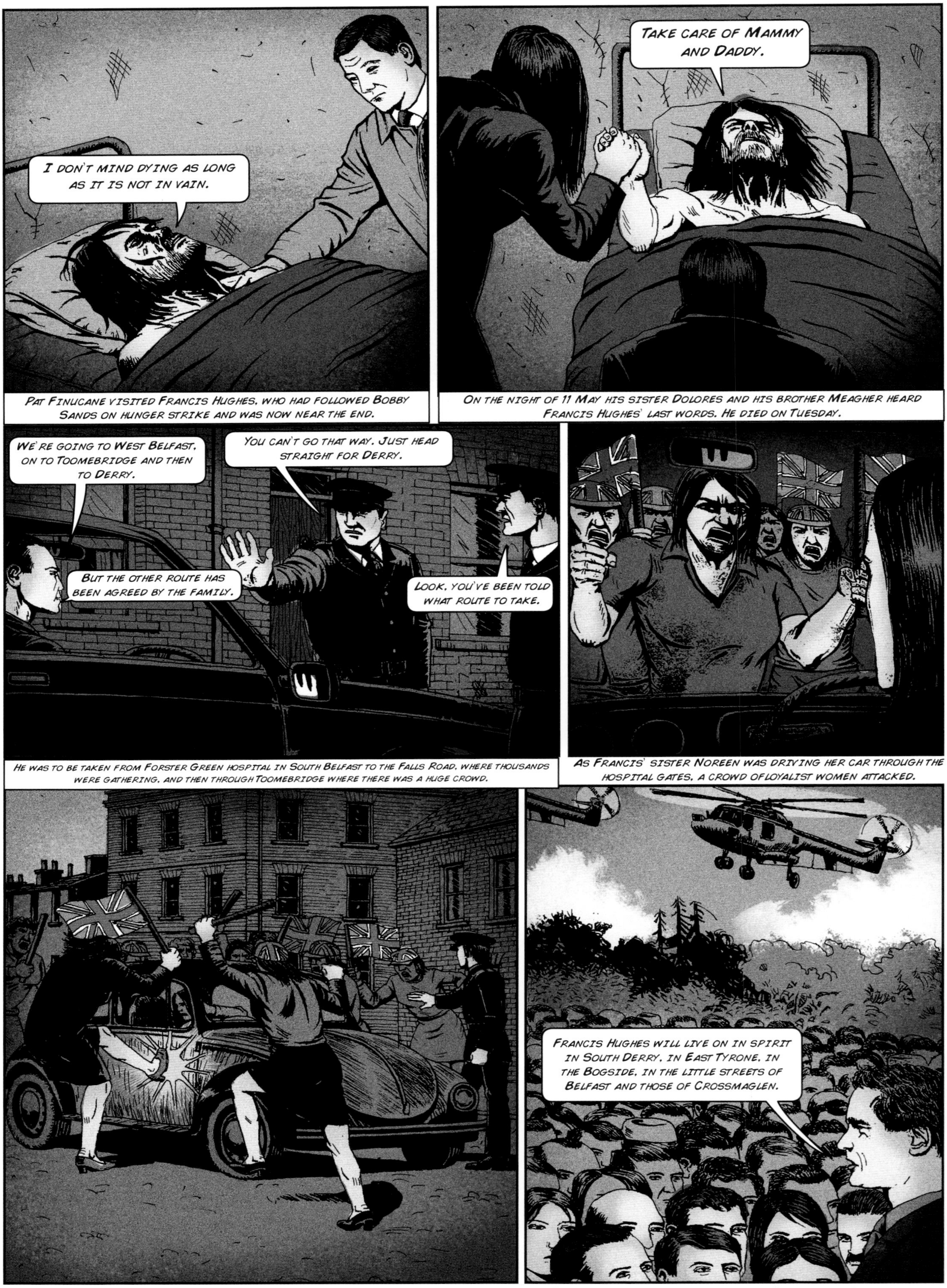
I DON'T MIND DYING AS LONG AS IT IS NOT IN VAIN.
PAT FINUCANE VISITED FRANCIS HUGHES, WHO HAD FOLLOWED BOBBY SANDS ON HUNGER STRIKE AND WAS NOW NEAR THE END.
TAKE CARE OF MAMMY AND DADDY.
ON THE NIGHT OF 11 MAY HIS SISTER DOLORES AND HIS BROTHER MEAGHER HEARD FRANCIS HUGHES' LAST WORDS. HE DIED ON TUESDAY.
WE'RE GOING TO WEST BELFAST, ON TO TOOMEBRIDGE AND THEN TO DERRY.
YOU CAN'T GO THAT WAY. JUST HEAD STRAIGHT FOR DERRY.
BUT THE OTHER ROUTE HAS BEEN AGREED BY THE FAMILY.
LOOK, YOU'VE BEEN TOLD WHAT ROUTE TO TAKE.
HE WAS TO BE TAKEN FROM FORSTER GREEN HOSPITAL IN SOUTH BELFAST TO THE FALLS ROAD, WHERE THOUSANDS WERE GATHERING, AND THEN THROUGH TOOMEBRIDGE WHERE THERE WAS A HUGE CROWD.
AS FRANCIS' SISTER NOREEN WAS DRIVING HER CAR THROUGH THE HOSPITAL GATES, A CROWD OF LOYALIST WOMEN ATTACKED.
FRANCIS HUGHES WILL LIVE ON IN SPIRIT IN SOUTH DERRY, IN EAST TYRONE, IN THE BOGSIDE, IN THE LITTLE STREETS OF BELFAST AND THOSE OF CROSSMAGLEN.

THEY THREW THEMSELVES AT HER CAR, HAMMERING THE WINDOWS AND ROOF AND WAVING UNION JACKS, AND STONES WERE HURLED AS THE POLICE LED THE CORTEGE THROUGH.

FRANCIS HUGHES WAS BURIED ON FRIDAY 15 MAY, AND AS THREE HELICOPTERS ROARED OVERHEAD, MARTIN MCGUINNESS DELIVERED THE ORATION TO A PACKED ATTENDANCE.

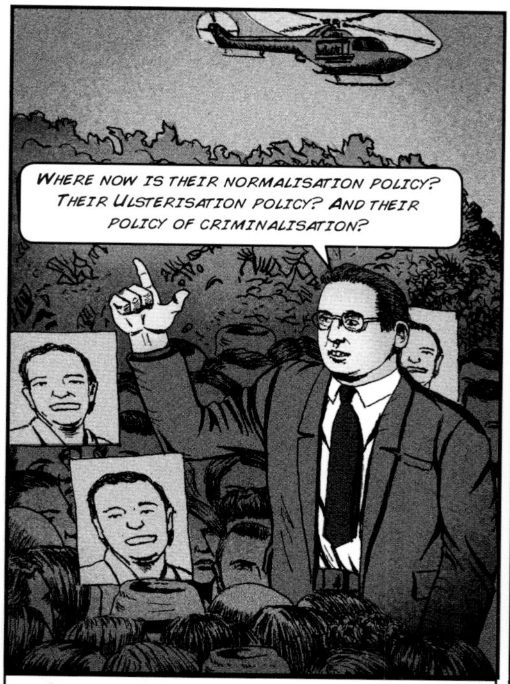
WHERE NOW IS THEIR NORMALISATION POLICY? THEIR ULSTERISATION POLICY? AND THEIR POLICY OF CRIMINALISATION?
RAYMOND MCCREESH DIED 21 MAY 1981 AND WAS BURIED ON AN ARMAGH HILLSIDE. RUAIRÍ Ó BRÁDAIGH GAVE THE ORATION AT THE GRAVESIDE.

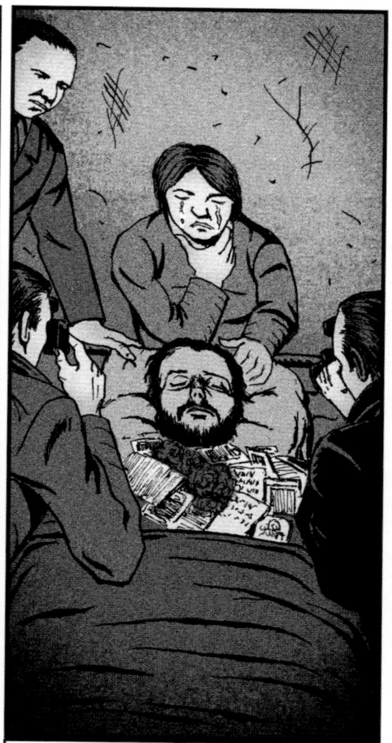
PATSY O'HARA DIED THE SAME DAY. HIS BROKEN NOSE AND WHAT LOOKED LIKE CIGARETTE BURNS WERE PHOTOGRAPHED.

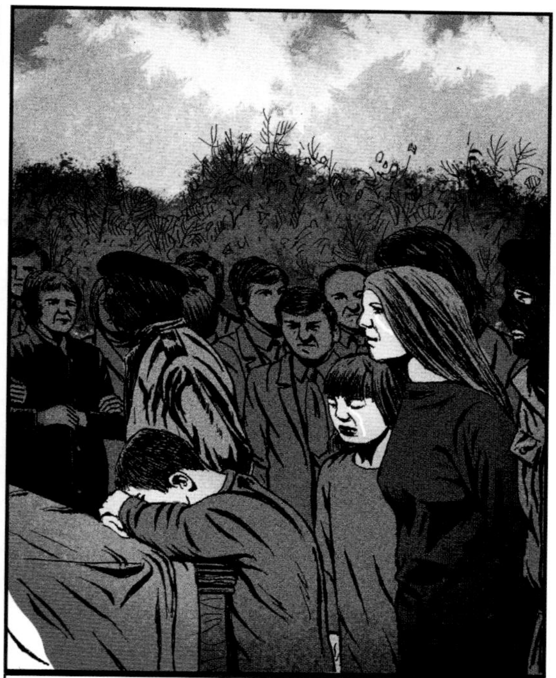
JOE MCDONNELL DIED ON 8 JULY '81. HE WAS BURIED IN THE NEW REPUBLICAN PLOT IN MILLTOWN CEMETERY NEXT TO BOBBY SANDS.

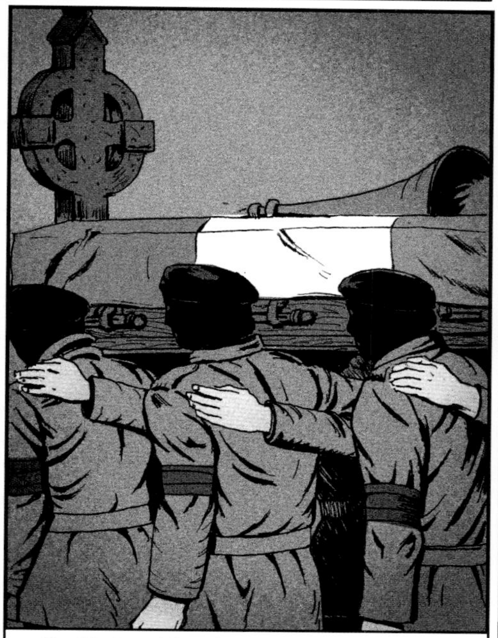
ON 13 JULY '81, MARTIN HURSON FINALLY PASSED AWAY. HE WAS BURIED AT ST. JOHN'S CHAPEL NEAR HIS HOME IN CAPPAGH.

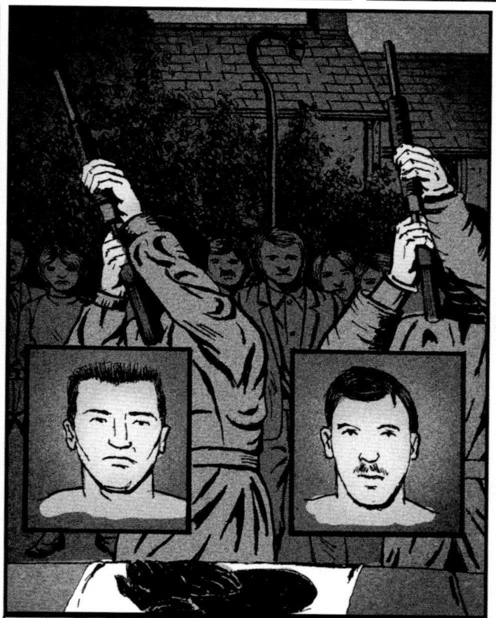
ON 1 AUGUST '81, KEVIN LYNCH DIED, AND KIERAN DOHERTY THE FOLLOWING DAY. KEVIN WAS BURIED IN DUNGIVEN AND KIERAN IN THE REPUBLICAN PLOT IN MILLTOWN CEMETERY.

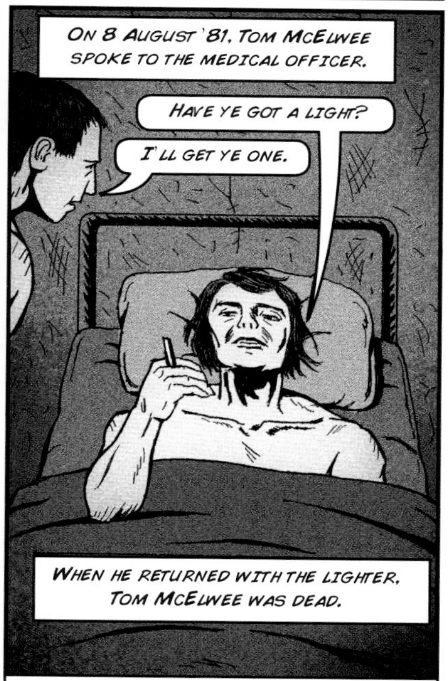
ON 8 AUGUST '81, TOM MCELWEE SPOKE TO THE MEDICAL OFFICER.
HAVE YE GOT A LIGHT?
I'LL GET YE ONE.
WHEN HE RETURNED WITH THE LIGHTER, TOM MCELWEE WAS DEAD.
HIS COFFIN WAS CARRIED BY HIS EIGHT SISTERS TO ST. MARY'S CHURCH IN BELLAGHY.

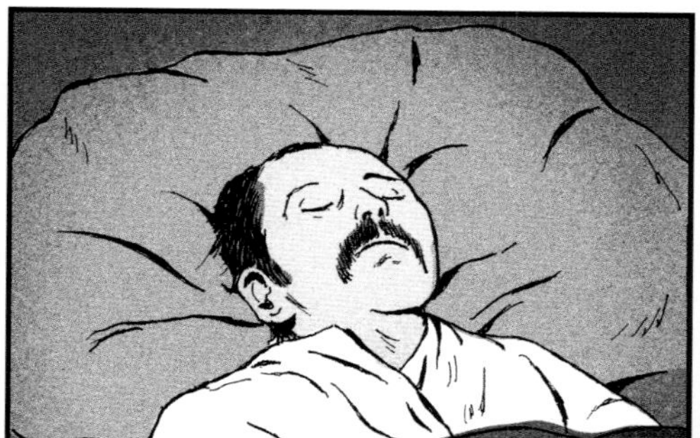
MICHAEL DEVINE DIED ON 20 AUGUST 1981. HE WAS THE LAST OF THE TEN HUNGER STRIKERS TO DIE.

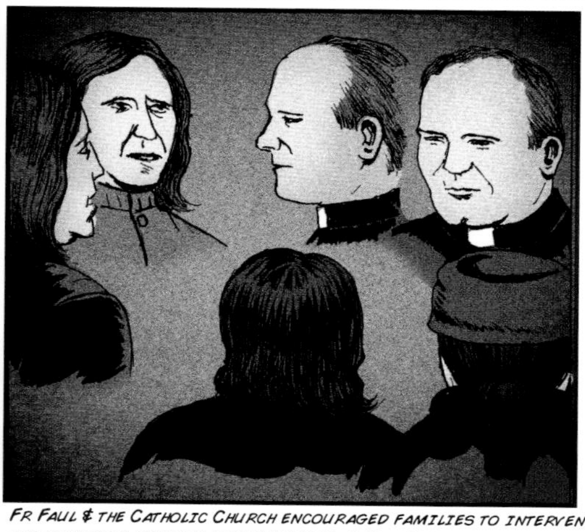
FR FAUL & THE CATHOLIC CHURCH ENCOURAGED FAMILIES TO INTERVENE AND SANCTION MEDICAL INTERVENTION WHEN THEIR SONS LAPSED INTO COMAS. THIS HAPPENED MORE AND MORE UNTIL THE HUNGER STRIKE AS A WEAPON WAS UNDERMINED. ON 3 OCTOBER, AFTER SEVEN MONTHS AND THE DEATHS OF TEN HUNGER STRIKERS, THE STRIKE WAS CALLED OFF.

THE PRISON PROTESTS CONTINUED UNTIL WITHIN A FEW YEARS THE BRITISH RESTORED POLITICAL STATUS. IN 1983 THE IRA TOOK OVER H-BLOCK 7 AND 37 PRISONERS SHOT THEIR WAY OUT THE JAIL. AMONG THEM WAS BRENDAN 'BIK' MCFARLANE. BOBBY SANDS' ELECTION ENCOURAGED SINN FÉIN TO TAKE PART IN ELECTIONS. THIS DUAL STRATEGY OF COMBINING ARMED STRUGGLE AND POLITICS WAS CALLED – 'THE ARMALITE AND THE BALLOT BOX' CAMPAIGN. IN THE 1990S GERRY ADAMS AND JOHN HUME HELD SECRET TALKS AND EXPLORED THE POSSIBILITY OF A PEACE PROCESS.

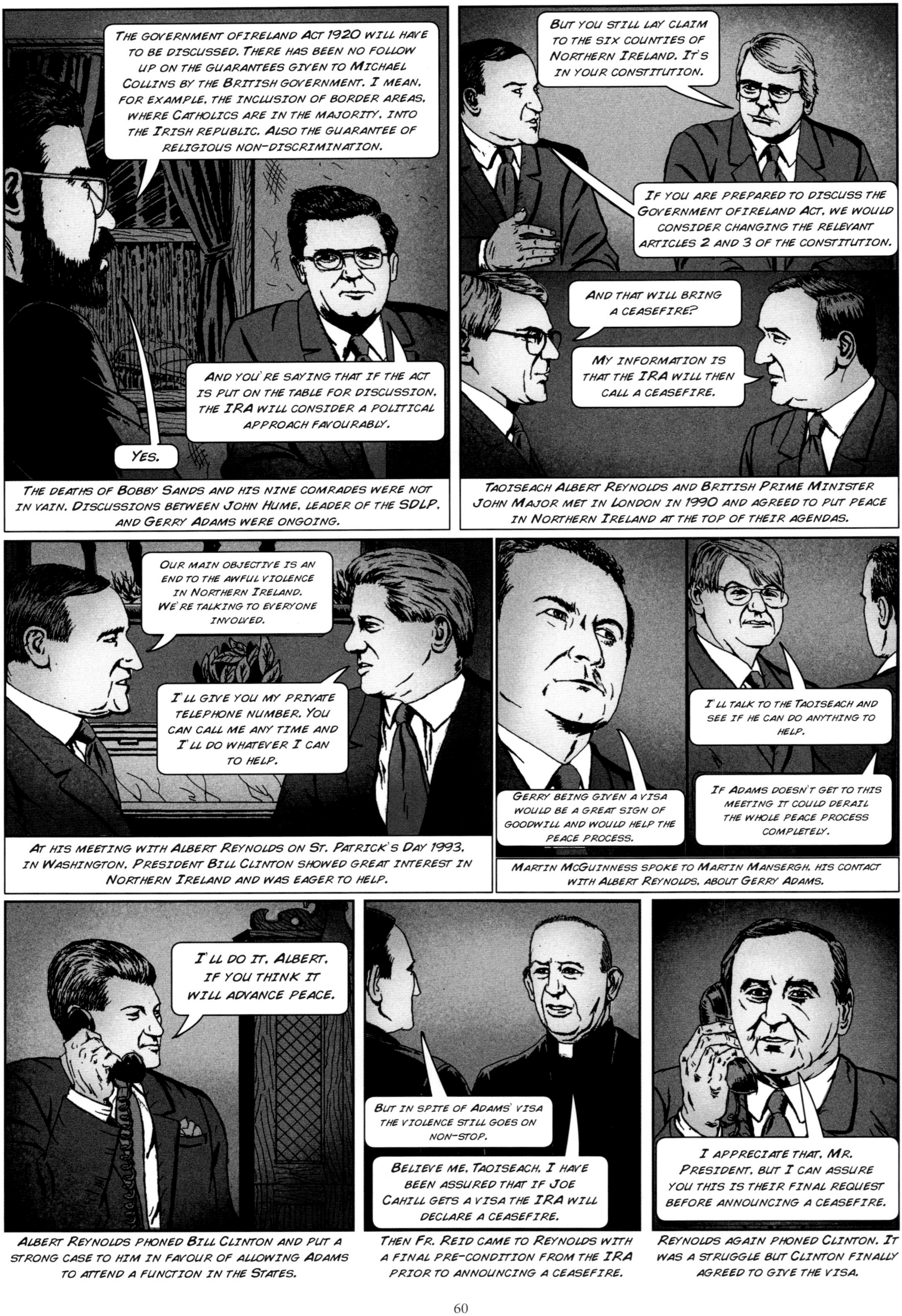
THE GOVERNMENT OF IRELAND ACT 1920 WILL HAVE TO BE DISCUSSED. THERE HAS BEEN NO FOLLOW UP ON THE GUARANTEES GIVEN TO MICHAEL COLLINS BY THE BRITISH GOVERNMENT. I MEAN, FOR EXAMPLE, THE INCLUSION OF BORDER AREAS, WHERE CATHOLICS ARE IN THE MAJORITY, INTO THE IRISH REPUBLIC. ALSO THE GUARANTEE OF RELIGIOUS NON-DISCRIMINATION.
AND YOU'RE SAYING THAT IF THE ACT IS PUT ON THE TABLE FOR DISCUSSION, THE IRA WILL CONSIDER A POLITICAL APPROACH FAVOURABLY.
YES.
THE DEATHS OF BOBBY SANDS AND HIS NINE COMRADES WERE NOT IN VAIN. DISCUSSIONS BETWEEN JOHN HUME, LEADER OF THE SDLP, AND GERRY ADAMS WERE ONGOING.
BUT YOU STILL LAY CLAIM TO THE SIX COUNTIES OF NORTHERN IRELAND. IT'S IN YOUR CONSTITUTION.
IF YOU ARE PREPARED TO DISCUSS THE GOVERNMENT OF IRELAND ACT, WE WOULD CONSIDER CHANGING THE RELEVANT ARTICLES 2 AND 3 OF THE CONSTITUTION.
AND THAT WILL BRING A CEASEFIRE?
MY INFORMATION IS THAT THE IRA WILL THEN CALL A CEASEFIRE.
TAOISEACH ALBERT REYNOLDS AND BRITISH PRIME MINISTER JOHN MAJOR MET IN LONDON IN 1990 AND AGREED TO PUT PEACE IN NORTHERN IRELAND AT THE TOP OF THEIR AGENDAS.
OUR MAIN OBJECTIVE IS AN END TO THE AWFUL VIOLENCE IN NORTHERN IRELAND. WE'RE TALKING TO EVERYONE INVOLVED.
I'LL GIVE YOU MY PRIVATE TELEPHONE NUMBER. YOU CAN CALL ME ANY TIME AND I'LL DO WHATEVER I CAN TO HELP.
AT HIS MEETING WITH ALBERT REYNOLDS ON ST. PATRICK'S DAY 1993, IN WASHINGTON, PRESIDENT BILL CLINTON SHOWED GREAT INTEREST IN NORTHERN IRELAND AND WAS EAGER TO HELP.
GERRY BEING GIVEN A VISA WOULD BE A GREAT SIGN OF GOODWILL AND WOULD HELP THE PEACE PROCESS.
I'LL TALK TO THE TAOISEACH AND SEE IF HE CAN DO ANYTHING TO HELP.
IF ADAMS DOESN'T GET TO THIS MEETING IT COULD DERAIL THE WHOLE PEACE PROCESS COMPLETELY.
MARTIN MCGUINNESS SPOKE TO MARTIN MANSERGH, HIS CONTACT WITH ALBERT REYNOLDS, ABOUT GERRY ADAMS.
I'LL DO IT, ALBERT, IF YOU THINK IT WILL ADVANCE PEACE.
ALBERT REYNOLDS PHONED BILL CLINTON AND PUT A STRONG CASE TO HIM IN FAVOUR OF ALLOWING ADAMS TO ATTEND A FUNCTION IN THE STATES.
BUT IN SPITE OF ADAMS' VISA THE VIOLENCE STILL GOES ON NON-STOP.
BELIEVE ME, TAOISEACH, I HAVE BEEN ASSURED THAT IF JOE CAHILL GETS A VISA THE IRA WILL DECLARE A CEASEFIRE.
THEN FR. REID CAME TO REYNOLDS WITH A FINAL PRE-CONDITION FROM THE IRA PRIOR TO ANNOUNCING A CEASEFIRE.
I APPRECIATE THAT, MR. PRESIDENT, BUT I CAN ASSURE YOU THIS IS THEIR FINAL REQUEST BEFORE ANNOUNCING A CEASEFIRE.
REYNOLDS AGAIN PHONED CLINTON. IT WAS A STRUGGLE BUT CLINTON FINALLY AGREED TO GIVE THE VISA.

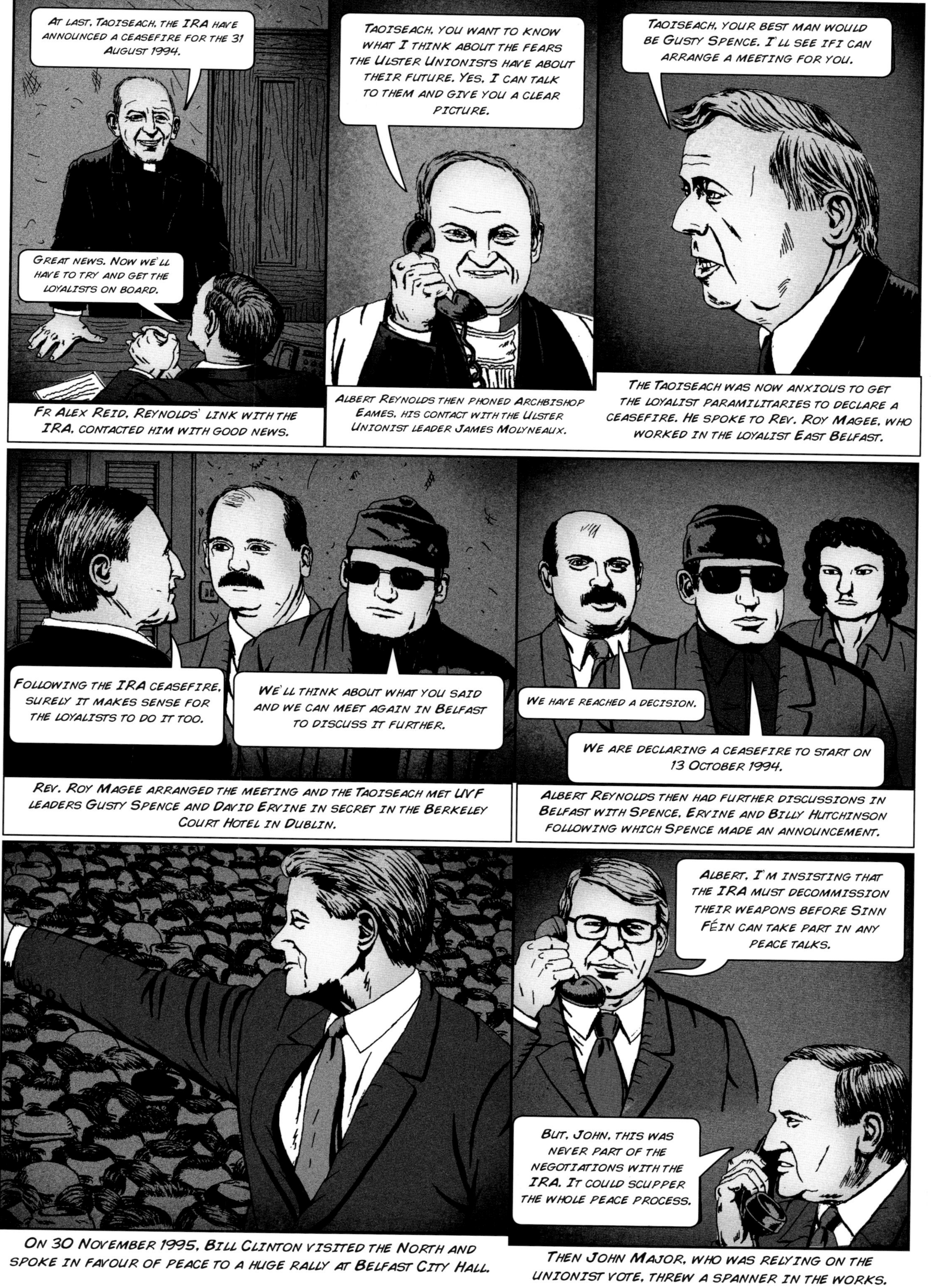
At last, Taoiseach, the IRA have announced a ceasefire for the 31 August 1994.
Great news. Now we'll have to try and get the loyalists on board.
Fr Alex Reid, Reynolds' link with the IRA, contacted him with good news.
Taoiseach, you want to know what I think about the fears the Ulster Unionists have about their future. Yes, I can talk to them and give you a clear picture.
Albert Reynolds then phoned Archbishop Eames, his contact with the Ulster Unionist leader James Molyneaux.
Taoiseach, your best man would be Gusty Spence. I'll see if I can arrange a meeting for you.
The Taoiseach was now anxious to get the loyalist paramilitaries to declare a ceasefire. He spoke to Rev. Roy Magee, who worked in the loyalist East Belfast.
Following the IRA ceasefire, surely it makes sense for the loyalists to do it too.
We'll think about what you said and we can meet again in Belfast to discuss it further.
Rev. Roy Magee arranged the meeting and the Taoiseach met UVF leaders Gusty Spence and David Ervine in secret in the Berkeley Court Hotel in Dublin.
We have reached a decision.
We are declaring a ceasefire to start on 13 October 1994.
Albert Reynolds then had further discussions in Belfast with Spence, Ervine and Billy Hutchinson following which Spence made an announcement.
On 30 November 1995, Bill Clinton visited the North and spoke in favour of peace to a huge rally at Belfast City Hall.
Albert, I'm insisting that the IRA must decommission their weapons before Sinn Féin can take part in any peace talks.
But, John, this was never part of the negotiations with the IRA. It could scupper the whole peace process.
Then John Major, who was relying on the unionist vote, threw a spanner in the works.

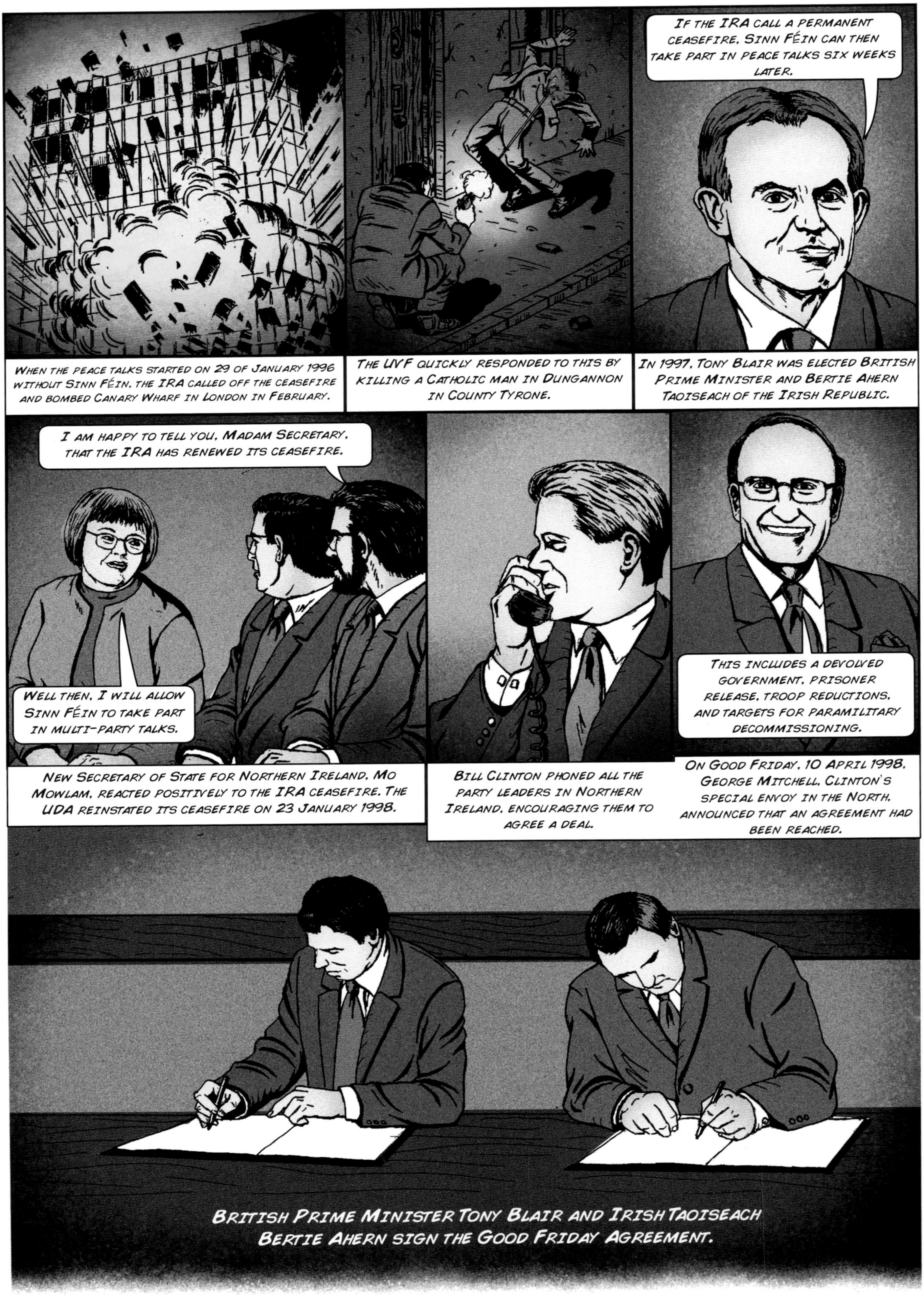
When the peace talks started on 29 of January 1996 without Sinn Féin, the IRA called off the ceasefire and bombed Canary Wharf in London in February.
The UVF quickly responded to this by killing a Catholic man in Dungannon in County Tyrone.
If the IRA call a permanent ceasefire, Sinn Féin can then take part in peace talks six weeks later.
In 1997, Tony Blair was elected British Prime Minister and Bertie Ahern Taoiseach of the Irish Republic.
I am happy to tell you, Madam Secretary, that the IRA has renewed its ceasefire.
Well then, I will allow Sinn Féin to take part in multi-party talks.
New Secretary of State for Northern Ireland, Mo Mowlam, reacted positively to the IRA ceasefire. The UDA reinstated its ceasefire on 23 January 1998.
Bill Clinton phoned all the party leaders in Northern Ireland, encouraging them to agree a deal.
This includes a devolved government, prisoner release, troop reductions, and targets for paramilitary decommissioning.
On Good Friday, 10 April 1998, George Mitchell, Clinton's special envoy in the North, announced that an agreement had been reached.
British Prime Minister Tony Blair and Irish Taoiseach Bertie Ahern sign the Good Friday Agreement.